WILLIAMS-SONOMA

Entertaining

INSPIRED MENUS FOR COOKING WITH FAMILY AND FRIENDS

RECIPES AND FOOD STYLING

George Dolese

GENERAL EDITOR

Chuck Williams

PHOTOGRAPHY

Quentin Bacon

Maren Caruso

Prue Ruscoe

STYLING

Sara Slavin

TEXT

Steve Siegelman

Oxmoor
House®

MENUS FOR SPRING

MENUS FOR SUMMER

CONTENTS

MENUS FOR AUTUMN

MENUS FOR WINTER

A FEAST OF INSPIRATIONS

For many people, there is something intimidating about the word "entertaining." The idea is appealing—a gathering of family or friends at your home to enjoy your food and one another's company—but putting it into action can be stressful and time-consuming. You must plan the party, create the menu, do the shopping, clean the house, cook for hours, and, of course, play the host. What if, after all that, the party does not turn out perfectly? Would it not be easier to get together at a restaurant?

It is time to set such concerns aside. Perhaps the first thing to do is to exchange the word "entertaining" for a less-intimidating, and thus less-stress-prompting, phrase: "having people over." Take away the stress and, suddenly, entertaining is not about being a style-setter, a caterer, or the perfect host. Instead, it can be about creating and sharing a happy occasion that reflects who you are. More important, however, is that you can have fun doing it.

This book holds the secrets to sidestepping the stress of entertaining and moving directly to the enjoyment. It is a collection of great ideas that add up to memorable occasions—all of them designed for hosts with busy lives. Included are scores of easy-to-make recipes that minimize last-minute pressure in the kitchen and maximize flavor at the table, and dozens of simple party touches—imaginative centerpieces, colorful decorative elements, and attractive table settings—that are guaranteed to create the ideal mood for celebration.

The recipes and ideas are grouped into sixteen occasions that highlight the flavors of spring, summer, autumn, and winter. But you can shuffle them as you like all year long to suit the realities of your life and your personal style. I encourage you to think of this book not as a series of prescriptions for perfect parties, but rather as a feast of inspirations that will inspire you to "have people over" more often.

PLANNING A PARTY

You have made the decision to host a party. Now, you need to work toward making it a manageable, stress-free, and, most important, pleasurable experience. The secret to making your party enjoyable for you as well as your guests is to stay organized and to tackle the major decisions one at a time.

A Reason to Celebrate

Planning any party, no matter how small or elaborate, begins with the simple question, "What is being celebrated?" Reasons for entertaining vary widely. You might want to mark a holiday or a special occasion, commemorate an accomplishment, a milestone, or an announcement, or repay an invitation. Settle on the "why" behind a party, and you will put all the decisions that follow into perspective. Even though the "why" may seem obvious, and may be as simple as "getting together with friends," put it into words. Write it at the top of a notepad page, and your planning has formally begun.

The first task is to set the date for the party. An easy way to ensure that entertaining is fun for both you and your company is to be realistic, especially when it comes to time. As you look at your calendar, consider not only the best date and time for your party, but also the days and hours on either side of your selection. If you work during the week, a Saturday evening is a great choice, because it gives you a day to get ready and—just as important—a day to recover. Three-day weekends are usually ideal for daytime parties. For weeknights, keep things casual, with simple, satisfying food that can be made in advance and easily served—and cleaned up.

Deciding on a Style

Next, determine the style of your party. Do you envision an informal gathering or an elaborate event? When making the decision, take into account your time, space, budget, and the number of guests—all concerns that are more critical to deciding on the style than what you are celebrating. If the style suits you, the party will be a success.

Casual entertaining is about creating a mood of relaxation and comfort that is carried through every aspect of the party. Even the most informal party can be a gracious occasion and festive celebration. The seating arrangements and table setting should be simple, and the menu should reflect that spirit with imaginative but unintimidating food and drink. For tips on setting an informal table see page 312. Both buffet service and family-style service (see page 12) work well for casual entertaining, and allow you to spend more time enjoying the company of your guests and less time in the kitchen.

PARTY-PLANNING CHECKLIST

- Pick a reason
- Set a date
- Determine the style
- Invite the guests
- Create the ambience
- Prepare the menu
- Relax and enjoy the party

TIMING THE INVITATION

CASUAL DINNER OR PARTY

Invitation should arrive at least one week in advance

FORMAL OR LARGE PARTY

Invitation should arrive at least two weeks in advance

HOLIDAY OR SPECIAL-OCCASION PARTY

Invitation should arrive one month in advance

Formal entertaining can produce a memorable event, especially for a holiday or special occasion. A formal table is generally elegant, fitted out with a tablecloth and the best accoutrements you can muster. The menu is usually more refined than that of a casual get-together, and the food is either plated in the kitchen for serving or arranged on an attractively appointed buffet. (For more information on setting a formal table, see page 313.) Consider drawing up a seating chart and setting out place cards, too, a particularly nice touch for any seated party. Keep this basic principle in mind, however: Nothing about a formal party should overwhelm the guests or the host. Elegance is less about extravagance than it is about simplicity and quality.

Whether you have a formal dining room or a table tucked into a corner of the kitchen, your house or apartment can work for entertaining. How you use the space at hand is what is important, and a little creativity can often produce remarkable results. For example, whether or not your table is too small to seat everyone, you might choose to use it for setting up a buffet and arrange other areas for eating, such as the living room, a kitchen island, a deck, or the backyard. Reinventing spaces for entertaining adds an element of creativity that helps put your guests in a party mood. You don't need a bigger space or a better one—any space will work if you have a good plan. On the following pages you will find ideas for an array of party styles, from ultra-formal to very casual and everything in between.

The Guest List and Invitations

You probably already have some people in mind to invite. Write down their names, and then begin rounding out the list by adding other people with both similar and different interests and backgrounds. If your party will be appropriate for children, invite enough kids to make up a group that will keep them all engaged. Once you have given thought to the timing and the space you have available, you should have a good idea of how many guests to invite. Settle on a target number, and after you've completed your list, jot down a few extra names in case you need to invite more people later.

There's no right or wrong way to invite guests. But keep in mind that the moment the invitation is received, it sets the tone of the party. E-mails and phone calls are easy and effective, especially for casual entertaining. Invitations sent through the mail make any event seem more special. They are particularly appropriate when a theme or special occasion is involved, or a lot of information must be conveyed, such as who is being honored, and whether gifts are permitted.

Mailed invitations do not need to be formal or expensive, however. They can be as simple as a handwritten note on a card that fits the style of your party. It is never inappropriate—and always helpful—to include RSVP (please reply), followed by your telephone number and/or e-mail address. Knowing in advance who will attend the party helps you plan shopping, cooking, and seating, and allows you to invite more guests as needed.

Planning the Menu

When you have settled on the scope and style of your party, it is time to move on to the menu. This may seem like a big hurdle, especially if you are an inexperienced cook, but it is not as difficult as you might think. That's because the decisions you have made about the occasion, guests, and style have largely defined and focused the menu already. As you start to select which recipes to prepare, three simple questions will help: What is the occasion? What is in season? What is realistic?

The occasion sets the tone of the food. Holidays, for example, often call for traditional recipes. Formal meals usually include more than one course, while casual entertaining generally requires fewer dishes. It's helpful to remember that most recipes can be made to work for all kinds of gatherings. Carrot Soup with Bacon and Chestnut Cream (page 227) served in a fine porcelain bowl and topped with a special garnish makes a festive first course for an elegant dinner, but it can also be served in rustic pottery soup plates with a salad and bread for a casual supper. So, rather than thinking immediately about recipes, begin by asking yourself what kinds of contrasting and complementary flavors, colors, textures, and ingredients feel appropriate for the style and mood of your occasion.

Seasonality is perhaps the single most helpful guide in deciding what to serve at a party, which is why the menus in this book have been arranged by season. From asparagus in the spring to crab in the winter, choosing seasonal ingredients can do a lot

of the work of menu planning for you. Whether you prepare them to showcase their flavor or use them to create more elaborate dishes, you can't miss. Start with a visit to a good grocery store or farmers' market for inspiration. See what looks and tastes especially good, and jot down a few notes as you go. Think about what kinds of dishes fit the weather, too: chilled soup on a hot day, a hearty braise for a winter night.

Be realistic. Take a moment to evaluate how much time you'll have, your budget, your skill level, the number of guests, and the limitations of your kitchen. These constraints do not have to put a damper on your party, as long as you recognize them in advance and plan accordingly. Build in whatever shortcuts you need, including serving a store-bought appetizer or dessert or using ready-made ingredients such as puff pastry, pesto, or caramel sauce. Consider serving a main course that can be made ahead of time, and perhaps even asking friends to bring part of the meal. Remember that the more guests you invite, the simpler the menu should be.

For most parties, you'll want to offer guests a variety of beverage options. Begin with the basics: bottled water, wine, and beer. If you want to serve mixed drinks, you can set up a bar or a self-serve drink station (see Basic Bar Checklist, page 13). Consider also serving a signature cocktail that fits the mood of the party, like a Blended Mojito (page 97) or Kir Royal (page 115). Be sure to have some nonalcoholic drinks on hand as well. Tips for pairing wine with food follow on page 15.

SERVING STYLES

RESTAURANT-STYLE SERVICE

- Appropriate for more formal occasions
- Dishes are individually plated in the kitchen and brought to the table
- A good idea when you have a small table that cannot hold many platters

FAMILY-STYLE SERVICE

- Best suited to informal occasions
- Food is arranged on large platters and brought to the table
- Guests serve themselves at the table

BUFFET SERVICE

- Works well for both formal and casual meals, especially for larger groups
- Food is arranged on a sideboard or at multiple locations
- Guests serve themselves

COCKTAIL PARTIES

- Best suited to formal occasions, especially larger groups
- Food is passed on trays
- Good for people with busy schedules

Serving Styles

Once your menu is set, the next step is deciding how to serve it.

Restaurant-style service, in which dishes are individually plated in the kitchen, is appropriate for more formal occasions, and is also a good idea if you have a small table that cannot accommodate many communal platters. To vary the pace of the meal and provide a change of scene, consider serving dessert and coffee in another room.

Family-style service is best suited to informal occasions. The food is arranged on large platters and brought to the table, where guests serve themselves. If a platter is large or cumbersome, each guest can hold it while the person on his or her left takes some food, or the host can circulate around the table with it.

Buffet service, in which food is arranged on a table or sideboard and guests serve themselves, works well for both formal and casual meals. It is particularly effective for larger groups because it allows people to eat in areas other than the dining room. If possible, allow for some traditional seating for anyone who is more comfortable eating at a table. You do not need to serve all of the food in one place. Creating multiple food stations will help avoid traffic jams and encourage guests to mingle. For detailed guidelines, see The Buffet (page 314).

Cocktail parties offer several advantages, especially if you have a busy life. They allow you to invite a number of guests with less cooking and prep work than a sit-down meal, and you can set a time limit—usually between two and three hours—on the invitation. Cocktail parties can be casual or formal, intimate and low-key or crowded and lively. Think about what style feels right for the occasion and the space, and plan the menu and mood accordingly.

Drinks are the stars at cocktail parties, so offer a few cocktails that fit the theme, along with wine, beer, and a relatively full bar. Plan on two to three drinks per guest. Serve an assortment of finger foods, either passed, set out at food stations, or both. Keep food portions small, preferably each a single bite. Remember, also, you can never have too much ice or too many napkins.

Taking Care of the Details

Seating, even for a relatively informal party, is best not left as an afterthought or a last-minute improvisation. Start with the chairs. They do not need to match as long as they look good together. To create a more uniform look, consider buying slipcovers, or add cushions if what you have is not comfortable for extended sitting.

Next, make a seating plan. Assigned seating is not just an old-fashioned tradition. You'll find that a seating plan puts guests at ease, as it relieves them of the awkwardness of choosing their dining companions. It also gives you a chance to balance the table and encourage conversation.

On a fresh page of your notepad, draw a picture of the table with a box for each chair. Begin by placing the host at the head of the table, if there is only one host, or place the hosts at the head and foot of the table, if there are two. Tradition holds that a female guest of honor sits to the right of the male host, and a male guest of honor to the right of the female host. Now pencil in the remaining guests, moving them around as needed until you have a plan that feels right. If possible, alternate men and women, avoid seating couples together, and pair guests with common interests. Once you have worked out the seating arrangement, make a place card for each guest, or skip the place cards and have your plan discreetly at hand when it comes time to indicate where each guest should sit.

Lighting and *music* help set the mood and should be planned ahead of time. For evening parties, use a combination of electric lights and candlelight to flatter your guests and create an inviting ambience. Scent-free, dripless regular or votive candles, such as beeswax candles, are good choices.

Music should complement the occasion or theme. Select it in advance, so it is easy to manage during the party. Set the volume low at first, to keep the music from competing with conversation. You can raise the volume as the party gets livelier.

Staying Organized

As the main elements of your party begin to take shape, it is important to keep track of all the little organizational details and special touches that will bring everything together.

Make two lists, Shopping and Tasks, on separate pages of your notepad. Organize the shopping list into categories. Try to arrange the tasks list in chronological order so you do not forget last-minute items. It is also helpful to work out a basic cooking and serving timetable to help you keep everything on track. If you are serving buffet style, set out the platters, dishes, and serving utensils, and map out a plan for where everything will go.

Recruiting help is a good idea for parties of eight or more (including the hosts) and will give you more time with your guests. For large cocktail parties, hiring someone to tend bar is helpful, and the same person can assist with cleanup and other tasks.

Expect the unexpected. Even at the most well-organized party, accidents and

CALCULATING BEVERAGE QUANTITIES

BOTTLED WATER
1 quart or liter bottle for every 2 guests

WINE OR SPARKLING WINE
1 bottle for every 2 or 3 wine drinkers

BEER
2 or 3 bottles for every beer drinker

LIQUOR
1 quart or liter for every 10 to 12 drinkers

BASIC BAR CHECKLIST

- Vodka
- Gin
- Scotch and bourbon whiskeys
- Aperitifs such as Campari or Lillet
- Red and white wines
- Club soda and tonic
- Soft drinks and sparkling water
- Orange, pineapple, and cranberry juices
- Lemon and lime wedges
- Ice

unanticipated problems are bound to occur. The key is to stay calm and let the party flow naturally while you deal with the situation discreetly.

The most important thing to remember is that a party is all about enjoyment, and guests take their cue from the host.

Pairing Wine with Food

The last step in planning a party is to select wines, or other beverages, to complement the food. If you are unsure about pairing the correct wines with your dishes, enlist the help of a wine-savvy friend or a local wine merchant. Deciding which wines will work best with a meal is largely a matter of personal taste. Begin by setting aside hard-and-fast rules about pairing red or white

wines with various foods. Instead, think about how the character of the wine will complement the food.

When you taste a wine (or discuss it with your wine merchant), keep in mind four basic qualities: *Body*—does the wine feel light or heavy on the tongue? *Intensity*—is it bold and assertive, or delicate and mild? *General flavor*—what kinds of tastes and aromas does it bring to mind (citrus, berry, apple, oak)? *Flavor characteristics*—is it dry or fruity; what are its levels of acidity and astringency (tannin)? Now think about the foods you will be serving. Keep in mind that food and wine are most complementary when their qualities are either similar (a full-bodied red served with a slow-cooked meat dish) or contrasting (a sweet, light white

matched with a spicy dish). As a general rule, wines are better appreciated when they progress from light to heavy over the course of the meal, with whites served before reds, and dry wines before sweet ones.

Putting It All Together

Once you've filled your notepad with lists, notes, and sketches, you have completed the hardest work. With a good plan in hand, you can use the menus and ideas in the chapters that follow as inspiration to help you bring your blueprint to life. You'll also find plenty of additional entertaining guidelines, tips, and handy reference information starting on page 310. Put all the elements together, and you can't go wrong, so have fun and enjoy your party.

MATCHING FOOD AND WINE

TYPE OF FOOD	WINE MATCH
Salty snack foods	Sparkling wines *Champagne, Prosecco, California sparkling wine*
Spicy, salty, or smoked dishes	Fruity, low-alcohol wines *Riesling, Gewürztraminer, Pinot Gris, Pinot Noir*
Rich or fatty dishes	Full-bodied wines *Chardonnay, Merlot, Cabernet Sauvignon, Zinfandel, Syrah*
Highly acidic dishes	High-acid wines *Sauvignon Blanc, Zinfandel, Chianti*
Desserts	Sweet wines, with the wine at least as sweet as the dish *Sauternes, Vin Santo, Muscat*
Goat's-milk cheeses	High-acid white wines *California Sauvignon Blanc, Sancerre*
Double- or triple-crème cheeses	Fruity or sweet red wines *Young Pinot Noir, tawny Port*
Blue cheeses	Sweet white wines *Sauternes, late-harvest wines*

SPRING

MENUS FOR SPRING

SUNDAY GATHERING

Baby Beet Salad

Lemon-Garlic Chicken

Peppery Garden Beans

Herbed Mashed Potatoes

*Chocolate-Walnut Cake with
Caramel Sauce*

20

MIDWEEK SUPPER

Antipasto Tray

Tossed Greens with Shaved Fennel

*Penne with Italian Sausage, Spinach,
and Bread Crumbs*

Affogato

36

EASTER BRUNCH

Mimosas

Carrot Muffins with Cream Cheese Frosting

Eggs Benedict

*Roasted Asparagus and Morels
with Shallot Butter*

Berry Trifle

52

BON VOYAGE PARTY

Cherry Tomato and Fava Bean Salad

*North African Chicken Skewers
with Herbed Couscous*

Coconut Layer Cake

70

SUNDAY GATHERING

What makes this family supper special is its effortless balance of the festive and the familiar. It is served in the dining room with flowers, candles, linen napkins, and the best china in the house, touches that reflect the notion that sharing a good family meal is itself cause for celebration. But there is nothing "formal" about the occasion. Set without a tablecloth, the table reveals its rich natural

tones, which helps make the mood warm and relaxed. So does the menu of mostly comfort food, served family style from big white platters and bowls. Taken together, these elements deliver the kind of unhurried Sunday-table pleasures of which family memories are made.

MENU

Baby Beet Salad

Lemon-Garlic Chicken

Peppery Garden Beans

Herbed Mashed Potatoes

*Chocolate-Walnut Cake
with Caramel Sauce*

Fumé Blanc

TIPS FOR FAMILY-STYLE ENTERTAINING

- Set the table early in the day and lay out all the serving utensils.
- If serving a whole chicken or similar main dish, bring it to the dining room whole and carve it at the table.
- Accompany the dinner with purchased rolls or artisanal bread.
- Place the dessert on the sideboard to tempt appetites throughout the meal.

WORK PLAN

AT LEAST ONE DAY IN ADVANCE

Roast the beets and sugar the
walnuts for the salad

Season the chicken

Parboil the green and yellow beans

THE DAY OF THE PARTY

Marinate the beets for the salad

Bake the cake

JUST BEFORE SERVING

Assemble the salad

Roast the chicken and make the pan sauce

Sauté the beans

Boil and mash the potatoes

Drizzle the cake with the caramel sauce

EARLY SPRING CENTERPIECE

A simple idea—using multi-colored winter citrus fruits to anchor the first blossoms of spring—is all it takes to make this inventive centerpiece. You can reproduce it throughout the year with the hard fruits and flowers of other seasons.

choose a wide, low clear glass vase or container, so that the arrangement will be stable and will allow guests to see one another across the table.

insert one type of flower—the largest variety first and a single stem at a time— pushing the stems between the fruits to firmly anchor them.

fill the vase two-thirds full with a variety of citrus fruits, such as oranges, lemons, limes, and kumquats. Add water to come halfway up the sides of the vase.

add two or three other types of flowers in the same way at random intervals to round out the arrangement, creating a pleasing shape and a balance of color.

BABY BEET SALAD

Seek out baby beets in an array of colors, such as golden yellow, pale pink, and magenta red, for an eye-catching presentation. If you can find them, blood oranges contrast nicely with the earthy beets.

Preheat the oven to 375°F (190°C). If the beet greens are attached, cut them off, leaving about 1 inch (2.5 cm) of the stem of the beets intact, and reserve the greens for another use. Place the beets in a roasting pan along with the garlic, thyme, olive oil, and 3 tablespoons water, and toss to mix. Season with salt and pepper. Cover the pan with aluminum foil, and roast the beets until tender when pierced with a knife, 30–40 minutes. Let cool to room temperature. Using a wet kitchen towel, gently rub the beets to remove the skins. Cut each beet in half or into wedges and transfer to a bowl. (The beets can be prepared up to this point 1–2 days in advance, covered, and refrigerated.)

To make the sugared walnuts, in a bowl, toss the walnuts with the oil. Add the confectioners' sugar and toss to coat evenly. Heat a small frying pan over medium heat. Add the walnuts and sauté just until they start to brown and the sugar begins to caramelize, about 3 minutes. Transfer to a small plate and let cool. (The cooled walnuts can be stored in an airtight container at room temperature for up to 1 day.)

In a small bowl, whisk together the mustard and vinegar. Slowly stream in the extra-virgin olive oil while whisking vigorously to make a vinaigrette. Stir in the orange zest and season to taste with salt and pepper. Pour the vinaigrette over the beets, toss to coat, and let stand at room temperature for 2–4 hours.

Using a small, sharp knife, cut a slice off both ends of each orange to reveal the flesh. Working with 1 orange at a time, stand it upright on a cutting board and thickly slice off the peel and pith in strips, following the contour of the fruit. Holding the orange in one hand over a bowl, cut along either side of each section to release it from the membrane, letting the sections drop into the bowl. Repeat with the remaining oranges. Pour any juice in the bowl over the beets.

Scatter the arugula over a platter. Using a slotted spoon, remove the beets from the vinaigrette and arrange over the greens along with the orange sections, onion slices, and walnuts. Drizzle a little of the vinaigrette over the top. Garnish with parsley.

Serves 6

3 bunches mixed baby beets, 3–4 lb (1.5–2 kg) total weight

2 cloves garlic, sliced

4 fresh thyme sprigs

2 tablespoons olive oil

Coarse salt and freshly ground pepper

SUGARED WALNUTS

1/2 cup (2 oz/60 g) walnut pieces

1 teaspoon canola oil

2 teaspoons confectioners' (icing) sugar

1 teaspoon Dijon mustard

3 tablespoons balsamic vinegar

1/3 cup (3 fl oz/80 ml) plus 2 tablespoons extra-virgin olive oil

Grated zest of 1 orange

4 oranges, preferably blood oranges

3 cups (3 oz/90 g) arugula (rocket) leaves

1 red onion, thinly sliced

2 tablespoons chopped fresh flat-leaf (Italian) parsley

LEMON-GARLIC CHICKEN

4 cloves garlic, chopped

Grated zest of 1 lemon

1 tablespoon chopped fresh rosemary
or thyme

1 tablespoon fennel seeds

1/2 teaspoon red pepper flakes
(optional)

Coarse salt and freshly ground
black pepper

2 chickens, 31/2–4 lb (1.75–2 kg) each

11/2 cups (12 fl oz/375 ml) reduced-
sodium chicken broth

Roast chicken served family style not only makes guests feel at home, but is also solid proof that the simplest things are usually best. In this recipe, the chicken is seasoned at least a day in advance so that the meat is tender and full of flavor when it emerges from the oven.

Using a spice grinder or mini food processor, pulse together the garlic, lemon zest, rosemary, fennel seeds, red pepper flakes (if using), 4–5 teaspoons salt, and 2 teaspoons black pepper until a coarse paste forms.

Remove and discard the excess fat from the chickens' cavities. Rinse the chickens and pat dry with paper towels. Rub the garlic mixture evenly over the skin and inside the cavities of the chickens. Tuck the wings behind the back, and place the birds side by side in a large baking dish. Cover loosely with plastic wrap and refrigerate for at least 24 hours or for up to 3 days.

Remove the chickens from the refrigerator about 1 hour before roasting. Preheat the oven to 425°F (220°C).

Select a heavy roasting pan large enough to hold the 2 birds. Place on the stove top over high heat and heat until hot. Pat the chickens with paper towels to remove any excess surface moisture from the skin, and put them in the hot pan, breast side up. Place in the oven and roast for 30 minutes. Turn the chickens breast side down and continue to roast for 30 minutes longer. Turn the chickens breast side up and roast until an instant-read thermometer inserted into the thickest part of a thigh away from the bone registers 170°F (77°C), about 30 minutes longer. Transfer the chickens to a cutting board, tent with aluminum foil, and let rest for 15 minutes.

Meanwhile, using a large spoon, skim off the fat from the pan drippings and place the roasting pan on the stove top over medium heat. Add the broth and deglaze the pan, scraping up any brown bits from the pan bottom. Cook until reduced by half, about 15 minutes. Season with salt and black pepper. Pour the pan juices through a fine-mesh sieve into a small warmed serving bowl; keep warm.

Carve the chickens in the kitchen or at the table and arrange on a warmed platter. Serve at once. Pass the warm pan juices at the table.

Serves 6

PEPPERY GARDEN BEANS

Pea shoots, the tender leaves and spiraled tendrils of the pea plant, add a peppery accent to sautéed green and wax beans. They can be found in most Asian produce markets. If unavailable, substitute watercress.

Bring a large pot three-fourths full of salted water to a boil over high heat. Add the green and yellow beans and boil until half-cooked, 3–4 minutes. Drain the beans into a colander, refresh with cold water, and pat dry with paper towels. Set aside. (The beans can be prepared up to this point 1 day in advance, covered tightly, and refrigerated until needed.)

In a large frying pan or wok over medium heat, melt the butter. Add the green onions and sauté for 2 minutes to release their flavor. Add the pea shoots and cooked beans and continue to sauté, stirring constantly, until the beans are warmed through and the pea shoots are just tender, about 3 minutes longer.

Season the beans and pea shoots to taste with salt and pepper and transfer to a warmed serving bowl. Serve at once.

Coarse salt

1/2 lb (250 g) haricots verts or small Blue Lake green beans, trimmed

1/2 lb (250 g) yellow wax beans, trimmed

4 tablespoons (2 oz/60 g) unsalted butter

6 green (spring) onions, including tender green tops, chopped

1/2 lb (250 g) pea shoots or watercress, tough stems removed

Freshly ground pepper

HERBED MASHED POTATOES

Light, buttery mashed potatoes taste best when eaten shortly after cooking, so organize your time in the kitchen to make sure they do not sit too long before they are passed at the table.

In a large saucepan over high heat, combine the potatoes, 2 teaspoons salt, and water to cover by 2 inches (5 cm). Bring to a rapid boil, reduce the heat to medium, and cook, uncovered, until tender when pierced with a knife, about 20 minutes.

Drain the potatoes and transfer them to a large bowl. Using a potato masher, mash them while they are still piping hot.

Add the sour cream, butter, and herbs to the potatoes, and slowly pour in the hot half-and-half while stirring with a wooden spoon. Continue to stir until the potatoes are light and creamy. Season to taste with salt and pepper. Serve at once.

Each recipe serves 6

4 lb (2 kg) Yukon gold, red, or russet potatoes, peeled and cut into 1-inch (2.5-cm) cubes

Coarse salt

1/2 cup (4 oz/125 g) sour cream

1/2 cup (4 oz/125 g) unsalted butter, cut into 1-inch (2.5-cm) pieces, at room temperature

1/2 cup (3/4 oz/20 g) mixed chopped fresh herbs such as chives, dill, tarragon, and/or thyme, in any combination

1 cup (8 fl oz/250 ml) half-and-half (half cream), heated

Freshly ground pepper

CHOCOLATE-WALNUT CAKE WITH CARAMEL SAUCE

An everyday buttermilk cake becomes something special when flavored with chocolate, walnuts, and caramel. Cut and serve the cake at the table, drizzling it first with warmed caramel sauce and accompanying each slice with vanilla ice cream.

3/4 cup (6 oz/185 g) unsalted butter

3 oz (90 g) semisweet (plain) chocolate, coarsely chopped

1 1/4 cups (5 oz/155 g) walnut pieces, toasted (page 215)

1 1/2 cups (10 1/2 oz/330 g) superfine (caster) sugar

1 cup (5 oz/155 g) all-purpose (plain) flour

1/2 cup (1 1/2 oz/45 g) unsweetened cocoa powder

1 1/2 teaspoons baking soda (bicarbonate of soda)

1/4 teaspoon salt

2 large eggs

1 cup (8 fl oz/250 ml) buttermilk

2 teaspoons vanilla extract (essence)

1 1/2 cups (12 fl oz/375 ml) store-bought caramel sauce

Vanilla ice cream for serving

Preheat the oven to 350°F (180°C). Butter a 10-cup (2.5-l) Bundt pan. Dust with flour and tap out the excess.

In a saucepan over low heat, combine the butter and chocolate and melt slowly, stirring to combine. Remove from the heat and set aside.

Put the walnuts in a food processor and process until finely chopped. Alternatively, finely chop the walnuts by hand on a cutting board.

In a large bowl, stir together the superfine sugar, flour, chopped walnuts, cocoa powder, baking soda, and salt. Using an electric mixer on low speed, beat in the following ingredients one at a time: the chocolate mixture, eggs, buttermilk, and vanilla extract. Increase the speed to high and continue to beat until light and fluffy, about 3 minutes. Pour into the prepared pan.

Bake the cake until a toothpick inserted into the center comes out clean, 40–45 minutes. Transfer to a wire rack and let the cake cool in the pan for 1 hour. Tap the sides of the pan gently on the counter to loosen the cake. Invert a flat cake plate or pedestal plate over the pan and invert the plate and the pan together. Tap the bottom of the pan with your hand or the back of a knife, and then lift off the pan. (The cake can be baked and cooled up to 8 hours in advance. Store the cooled, unmolded cake, loosely wrapped with plastic wrap, at room temperature.)

Just before serving, pour the caramel sauce into a small pan and place over low heat until warm. Drizzle the warmed caramel over the cake. Cut the cake into slices, and accompany each slice with a scoop of vanilla ice cream.

Serves 8

MIDWEEK SUPPER

The secret to making weeknight entertaining work is a casual style of serving, a roomful of good friends, and an uncomplicated menu that includes a few store-bought items. This lively, Italian-inspired menu is easy to prepare and mostly assembled once the guests arrive, so inviting them to mingle over antipasto and Chianti in the kitchen while you cook is part of the fun. At the center of the meal is a hearty sausage-flecked pasta and a tossed salad. It can

be served in the kitchen and eaten anywhere—at the table, in comfy chairs in the living room, or even standing at the kitchen counter. Everyday flatware and colorful, modern dishes are right at home with this menu.

TIPS FOR CASUAL ENTERTAINING

- Keep store-bought items such as olives and marinated vegetables on hand for spur-of-the-moment hors d'oeuvres.

- Arrange plates and cutlery on a kitchen island or counter and let guests help themselves.

- Set up a beverage station in the kitchen for easy access.

- Use this menu, or a similar one, for a pre-event dinner.

MENU

Antipasto Tray

Tossed Greens with Shaved Fennel

*Penne with Italian Sausage, Spinach,
and Bread Crumbs*

Affogato

Chianti Classico

WORK PLAN

THE DAY OF THE PARTY

Purchase the meats and cheeses
for the antipasti

Shave the vegetables and make
the vinaigrette for the salad

JUST BEFORE SERVING

Warm the olives and arrange
the antipasto tray

Toss the salad

Make the penne dish

Brew espresso for the dessert

FLATWARE BUNDLES

Bundling flatware in a napkin adds style to a casual meal, especially one that is not served at a set table. Choose one of these three easy ideas and arrange the assembled bundles on a tray the night before.

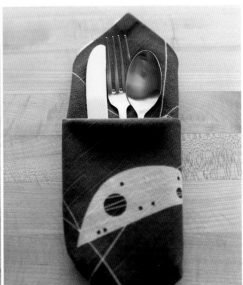

roll a napkin—after first folding it in half—around the flatware. Tie the bundle with natural twine or raffia. Turn down one corner of the napkin and tuck it under the twine.

fold a napkin into quarters, with the open points at the top. Fold the point of the top layer down to meet the bottom corner, to form a pocket. Fold the left and right corners under. Tuck the utensils into the pocket.

bundle flatware in the center of a quartered napkin, making a neat tie with a length of grosgrain or other cloth ribbon that complements the table.

ANTIPASTO TRAY

An antipasto tray is an easy-to-assemble starter for a midweek meal. Keep as many of the components as possible stored in the pantry so that all you have to do for the party is supplement with cheeses and meats. Serve with bread sticks and coarse country bread.

To make the olives, preheat the oven to 350°F (180°C). In a small baking dish, combine the olives, olive oil, fennel seeds, red pepper flakes, lemon zest, and ¼ teaspoon each salt and black pepper. Bake the olives until heated through, about 20 minutes. Transfer to a warmed small serving dish and keep warm.

Put the warm marinated olives, the artichokes, caperberries, roasted peppers, anchovies, and Parmesan pieces into separate small bowls or plates. Separate the slices of cured meats and layer them attractively on a plate.

Arrange the bowls and plates on a large serving tray along with some serving utensils. Serve at once.

Serves 6

WARM MARINATED OLIVES

1 cup (5 oz/155 g) mixed oil-cured green and black olives

2 tablespoons extra-virgin olive oil

2 teaspoons fennel seeds, crushed

¼ teaspoon red pepper flakes

Grated zest of 1 lemon

Coarse salt and freshly ground black pepper

¾ lb (375 g) marinated artichokes, drained

¼ lb (125 g) large caperberries

6 oz (185 g) roasted red bell peppers (capsicums), cut into narrow strips

3 oz (90 g) anchovy fillets

6 oz (185 g) Parmesan cheese, broken into bite-sized pieces

¾ lb (375 g) thinly sliced mixed Italian cured meats such as prosciutto, *coppa,* and *bresaola*

TOSSED GREENS WITH SHAVED FENNEL

Crunchy fennel and celery dressed in a light lemon vinaigrette give this simple green salad an Italian accent. If you have a mandoline, use it to shave the fennel and celery into thin, uniform, nearly transparent slices.

LEMON-GARLIC VINAIGRETTE

6 tablespoons (3 fl oz/90 ml) extra-virgin olive oil

3 tablespoons fresh lemon juice

1 clove garlic, minced

Coarse salt and freshly ground pepper

2 fennel bulbs, about 1¹/₂ lb (750 g) total weight

1 celery stalk

¹/₂ lb (250 g) mixed salad greens

To make the vinaigrette, in a small bowl, whisk together the olive oil, lemon juice, and garlic. Season to taste with salt and pepper. Let stand for 30 minutes to allow the flavors to blend.

Cut off the stems and feathery fronds of the fennel bulbs and remove any bruised or discolored outer leaves. Cut each bulb in half lengthwise and cut out any tough core portions. Cut the halves crosswise into paper-thin slices. Place the slices in a bowl, add the vinaigrette, and toss well. Cut the celery into paper-thin slices, add them to the bowl, and toss well. (The vegetables can be prepared up to this point, covered tightly, and refrigerated for up to 4 hours.)

Put the salad greens in a large bowl. Add the fennel and celery, with the vinaigrette, and toss to coat the greens evenly with the vinaigrette. Divide the salad among individual plates, or pass the bowl at the table.

Serves 6

PENNE WITH ITALIAN SAUSAGE, SPINACH, AND BREAD CRUMBS

Pasta dishes are often an ideal way to entertain during the week. Many require nothing more than assembling a few ingredients in a large bowl and tossing them together with just-cooked pasta. You can spice up the dish with hot, rather than mild, sausage.

Bring a large pot three-fourths full of salted water to a boil over high heat. Add the penne, stir well, and cook until al dente, about 10 minutes, or cook according to the package instructions.

Meanwhile, in a large frying pan over medium heat, warm the olive oil. Crumble the sausage into the pan and sauté until lightly browned and cooked through, about 5 minutes. Using a slotted spoon, transfer the sausage to a warmed large bowl.

Return the pan to medium-high heat, add the garlic to the pan, and sauté for 2–3 minutes to release its flavor. Pour in the red wine and deglaze the pan, scraping up any brown bits from the pan bottom. Transfer the garlic and the pan juices to the bowl holding the sausage. Add the spinach, sun-dried tomatoes, fennel seeds, red pepper flakes, and croutons to the bowl and cover to keep warm.

Drain the pasta, reserving about $1/2$ cup (4 fl oz/125 ml) of the pasta cooking water. Immediately transfer the pasta to the bowl holding the other ingredients and toss, adding the $1/2$ cup cheese, the cream, and the reserved pasta water.

Season the pasta to taste with salt and black pepper. Serve at once, passing additional cheese.

Serves 6

Coarse salt

1 lb (500 g) penne

2 tablespoons extra-virgin olive oil

$1^1/2$ lb (750 g) sweet Italian sausage, casings removed

2 cloves garlic, thinly sliced

$1/4$ cup (2 fl oz/60 ml) dry red wine

6 oz (185 g) baby spinach leaves

$1/2$ cup ($2^1/2$ oz/75 g) olive oil–packed sun-dried tomatoes, drained and chopped

2 teaspoons fennel seeds, crushed

$1/4$ teaspoon red pepper flakes

$1/2$ cup (2 oz/60 g) crushed seasoned croutons

$1/2$ cup (2 oz/60 g) shaved pecorino romano cheese, plus more for serving

$1/2$ cup (4 fl oz/125 ml) heavy (double) cream, warmed

Freshly ground black pepper

Ground dark-roast coffee for brewing espresso, or 1¹/₂ cups (12 fl oz/375 ml) hot double-strength brewed coffee

1 pt (16 fl oz/500 ml) premium vanilla or coffee ice cream

Store-bought cookies for serving (optional)

AFFOGATO

Affogato, which literally means "drowned," is the simplest of desserts. It calls for pouring a shot of hot espresso over a scoop of ice cream. Because each espresso must be brewed individually, you will not be able to serve all of your guests at the same time, but this party's casual atmosphere allows for staggered serving.

Using an espresso machine, and following the manufacturer's instructions, use the ground coffee to brew 6 shots of espresso, one at a time. While each shot is brewing, put a scoop of ice cream in a coffee cup or shallow dessert bowl. As each shot of espresso is ready, give it to a guest who then pours it over the serving of ice cream. Accompany each serving with a cookie, if desired, and serve at once.

If using double-strength brewed coffee, pour about ¹/₄ cup (2 fl oz/60 ml) of the hot coffee into each of 6 small coffee cups. Place a scoop of ice cream in each of 6 small bowls. Give 1 cup of coffee and 1 bowl of ice cream to each guest, who then pours the coffee over the ice cream. Accompany each serving with a cookie, if desired, and serve at once.

Serves 6

EASTER BRUNCH

Creating the right mood for an occasion can be as simple as selecting a few decorative elements and a color palette. Here, delicate lilies of the valley and Easter eggs in pastel shades set the tone for a leisurely Easter brunch, and everything else follows suit—from plates and table linens to decorative bowls filled with holiday candies.

The festive menu brings some of the best flavors and colors of springtime to the table. Although much of the food is made at serving time, it all holds well on a buffet set up on an enclosed patio. The same menu could also be served indoors as a traditional sit-down meal.

MENU

Mimosas

*Carrot Muffins with
Cream Cheese Frosting*

Eggs Benedict

*Roasted Asparagus and Morels
with Shallot Butter*

Berry Trifle

WORK PLAN

AT LEAST ONE DAY IN ADVANCE

Make the frosting for the carrot muffins

Make the trifle

THE DAY OF THE PARTY

Bake and frost the muffins

Make the hollandaise for the eggs Benedict

JUST BEFORE SERVING

Prepare the eggs Benedict

Roast the vegetables

Garnish the trifle

TIPS FOR OUTDOOR BUFFETS

- Arrange seating areas away from the buffet for better flow.

- Position food tables near the kitchen to make replenishing easier.

- If the weather is cool, have shawls or throws on hand to keep guests warm.

- Be prepared to shift indoors in case of inclement weather.

An Easter Egg Centerpiece

This colorful centerpiece creates a stylish focal point for the Easter buffet table. Use decorated eggs found during the morning hunt, arranging them on a bed of lilies of the valley on a simple pedestal plate.

color hard-boiled eggs in a variety of pastel tones made by mixing a few drops of food coloring with 2 cups (16 fl oz/500 ml) hot water and 1 teaspoon distilled white vinegar. Let them dry in egg cartons.

line the rim of a neutral-colored pedestal plate with stems of lily of the valley, allowing the leaves and flowers to drape over the edge. Cover the center of the plate with a cushioning layer of florists' moss.

arrange the eggs in a pyramid over the moss, randomly mixing the colors. Gently pull out some of the greenery from beneath the eggs to balance the presentation.

pour fresh orange juice into chilled Champagne flutes, filling each about one-third full. If desired, add orange liqueur.

fill the flutes with sparkling wine, pouring it in a slow, steady stream to keep the wine's bubbles in check.

garnish each glass with a quartered orange slice. You can either float it in the drink, or cut a slit in the flesh and balance it on the rim of the glass.

Mimosas

Sparkling wine mixed with freshly squeezed orange juice is an easy and festive cocktail for a weekend or holiday brunch. Any remaining wine can be kept on ice for guests desiring a second cocktail.

1 cup (8 fl oz/250 ml) plus 2 tablespoons
fresh orange juice, well chilled

6 tablespoons (3 fl oz/90 ml) orange
liqueur (optional)

2 bottles (24 fl oz/750 ml each)
Champagne or other sparkling wine,
well chilled

6 orange slice quarters

Put 6 Champagne flutes or wineglasses in the freezer to chill for at least 15 minutes. Pour 3 tablespoons orange juice and 1 tablespoon orange liqueur, if using, into each chilled flute. Slowly fill the flutes with the Champagne, then garnish each glass with an orange slice quarter.

Serves 6

Carrot Muffins with Cream Cheese Frosting

These bite-sized muffins can be assembled a few hours ahead so that they are ready when guests arrive. Arrange on a platter lined with a linen napkin—the fabric will help keep them in place. If you have the time, look for paper cup liners to complement the color scheme of your party.

To make the frosting, in a bowl, using an electric mixer on medium speed, beat together the cream cheese and confectioners' sugar until thoroughly blended, about 2 minutes. Add the orange zest and orange oil and continue to beat until fluffy, about 2 minutes longer. (The frosting can be made the night before serving and stored in the refrigerator in an airtight container; bring the frosting to room temperature before using.)

Preheat the oven to 350°F (180°C). Line 24 miniature muffin-pan cups with decorative paper liners.

In a bowl, combine the carrot, walnuts, pineapple, currants, coconut, and ¼ cup (1½ oz/45 g) of the flour, and set aside until needed. Sift together the remaining ¾ cup (3½ oz/110 g) flour, the cinnamon, ginger, baking powder, baking soda, and salt onto a piece of parchment (baking) paper; set aside.

In a large bowl, using the electric mixer on medium speed, beat together the butter and brown sugar until fluffy, about 4 minutes. Reduce the speed to low and add the eggs one at a time, beating well after each addition. Beat in the sour cream and then the vanilla extract. Slowly add the flour mixture and continue to mix just until the flour mixture is well incorporated, 1–2 minutes. Using a rubber spatula, lightly but thoroughly fold in the carrot mixture. Divide the batter evenly among the lined muffin cups, filling each cup about three-fourths full.

Bake the muffins until golden and a toothpick inserted into the center of a muffin comes out clean, 20–25 minutes. Transfer the muffin pans to a wire rack and let cool to room temperature.

Remove the cooled muffins from the pans. Up to 2 hours before serving, using a thin offset spatula, frost each muffin. Arrange on a platter and serve.

Makes 24 muffins; serves 6

CREAM CHEESE FROSTING

6 oz (185 g) cream cheese, at room temperature

⅓ cup (1½ oz/45 g) confectioners' (icing) sugar

Grated zest of 1 orange

¼ teaspoon orange oil

¼ cup (¾ oz/20 g) grated carrot

¼ cup (1 oz/30 g) finely chopped walnuts

¼ cup (1½ oz/45 g) drained, canned crushed pineapple

¼ cup (1½ oz/45 g) dried currants

¼ cup (1 oz/30 g) sweetened shredded dried coconut

1 cup (5 oz/155 g) all-purpose (plain) flour

1 teaspoon ground cinnamon

1 teaspoon ground ginger

1 teaspoon baking powder

¼ teaspoon baking soda (bicarbonate of soda)

¼ teaspoon salt

6 tablespoons (3 oz/90 g) unsalted butter, at room temperature

¾ cup (6 oz/185 g) firmly packed golden brown sugar

2 large eggs

½ cup (4 oz/125 g) sour cream

1 teaspoon vanilla extract (essence)

EGGS BENEDICT

This contemporary recipe for eggs Benedict calls for sliced honey-cured ham and toasted sourdough bread spread with a piquant green onion butter. Classic hollandaise is made foolproof by whisking cubes of chilled butter into the warm yolks, which helps keep the sauce from separating.

GREEN ONION BUTTER

1/2 cup (4 oz/125 g) unsalted butter, at room temperature

3 green (spring) onions, including tender green tops, minced

HOLLANDAISE SAUCE

6 large egg yolks

2 tablespoons whole milk

11/4 cups (10 oz/310 g) chilled unsalted butter, cut into 1/2-inch (12-mm) cubes

1/4 cup (2 fl oz/60 ml) fresh lemon juice

Coarse salt and cayenne pepper

11/2 lb (750 g) thinly sliced cooked honey-cured ham

12 slices sourdough bread

Coarse salt

2 tablespoons distilled white vinegar

12 eggs

4 green (spring) onions, including tender green tops, chopped

Paprika for sprinkling

To make the green onion butter, in a bowl, using a wooden spoon, mix together the butter and green onions until evenly blended. Set aside.

To make the hollandaise, in the top pan of a double boiler or in a heatproof bowl, whisk together the egg yolks and milk. Place the pan or bowl over (not touching) barely simmering water in the lower pan of the double boiler or in a saucepan and continue to whisk until warm and frothy, 4–5 minutes. Whisk in the butter pieces a few at a time, beating after each addition until fully incorporated before adding more. Continue to whisk until all the butter has been incorporated and the sauce is thick enough to coat the back of a spoon, 3–5 minutes total. Stir in the lemon juice and season with a pinch each of salt and cayenne pepper. The sauce can be kept warm over barely simmering water for up to 3 hours, stirring from time to time.

Preheat the oven to 200°F (95°C). Wrap the sliced ham in aluminum foil and place in the oven to warm. Toast the bread slices, then spread them lightly on both sides with the green onion butter. Keep warm until serving.

To poach the eggs, in a large frying pan, pour in water to a depth of about 1¹/2 inches (4 cm). Add 1 teaspoon salt and the vinegar and bring to a boil over high heat. Reduce the heat so that the water is just below boiling. Working quickly, and being careful not to crowd the pan, break an egg into a saucer and gently slip it into the water. Repeat with more eggs, keeping them well spaced. Cook just until the whites have set and the yolks are glazed over but still soft, 3–4 minutes. Using a skimmer or slotted spatula, carefully remove the eggs from the water, letting them drain well, and place on a plate; keep warm. Repeat with the remaining eggs.

To serve, place 2 toasted bread slices on each warmed individual plate. Top each slice with an equal amount of the ham, then place a poached egg in the center of each slice. Spoon an equal amount of the hollandaise sauce over each egg. Sprinkle the top with chopped green onion and paprika. Serve at once.

Serves 6

ROASTED ASPARAGUS AND MORELS WITH SHALLOT BUTTER

Look for thin asparagus spears for this dish; they are generally more tender, and the stalks do not require peeling before cooking. If you are unable to find morels, oyster mushrooms or common brown mushrooms, also known as cremini, are a good substitute.

Preheat the oven to 450°F (230°C).

Place the asparagus on a rimmed baking sheet large enough to hold them in a single layer. Brush the morels clean. If there is a lot of grit or other dirt lodged in their honeycomblike surface, you may need to dunk them briefly in cold water to free it; then pat dry with paper towels. If the morels are large, cut them crosswise into rings ¼ inch (6 mm) wide. Leave small ones whole. Add the mushrooms to the baking sheet holding the asparagus.

In a small saucepan over low heat, melt the butter. Add the shallots and sauté for 1 minute to release their flavor. Drizzle the shallot butter evenly over the asparagus and morels. Scatter the tarragon over the top and season with salt and pepper. Using your hands, toss the asparagus and morels in the butter and tarragon until evenly coated, then spread them into a single layer again.

Roast until the asparagus is lightly browned but still crisp and the morels are dark brown, about 10 minutes. Transfer the asparagus and morels to a serving platter and drizzle any pan juices over the top. Serve at once.

Serves 6

1½ lb (750 g) thin asparagus spears, tough ends removed

¼ lb (125 g) fresh morel mushrooms

4 tablespoons (2 oz/60 g) unsalted butter

2 shallots, minced

1 tablespoon chopped fresh tarragon

Coarse salt and freshly ground pepper

2 lb (1 kg) mixed berries such as strawberries, raspberries, blackberries, and blueberries, in any combination, plus more whole berries for garnish

1/4 cup (1 3/4 oz/55 g) superfine (caster) sugar

1/4 cup (2 fl oz/60 ml) fresh orange juice

1/4 cup (2 fl oz/60 ml) orange liqueur

1 lemon pound cake, 9-inch (23-cm) loaf

2 cups (16 fl oz/500 ml) heavy (double) cream

1/4 cup (1 oz/30 g) confectioners' (icing) sugar

1 1/2 teaspoons vanilla extract (essence)

1/2 lb (250 g) mascarpone cheese, at room temperature

Grated zest of 1 lemon

Fresh mint sprigs for garnish

BERRY TRIFLE

Although seemingly elaborate, trifle is quick to assemble when you use store-bought pound cake. Mascarpone cheese folded into sweetened whipped cream adds a layer of rich, silky indulgence. You can also use sliced apricots, peaches, and plums in place of the berries.

If using strawberries, hull and slice them. Place them in a bowl and add the other berries. Add the superfine sugar, orange juice, and liqueur and stir gently to mix. Set aside to macerate for at least 1 hour or for up to 3 hours.

Cut the pound cake into 1-inch (2.5-cm) cubes and set aside until ready to assemble the trifle. You should have about 6 cups (1 lb/500 g).

In a large bowl, using an electric mixer on medium-high speed, whip together the cream, confectioners' sugar, and vanilla extract until soft peaks form, about 3 minutes. In a separate bowl, using clean beaters and with the mixer on medium-high speed, whip the mascarpone until soft. Using a rubber spatula, fold the whipped mascarpone and the lemon zest into the whipped cream until the mixture is evenly blended.

Select a footed glass trifle bowl 9–10 inches (23–25 cm) in diameter and 5 inches (13 cm) deep. Alternatively, use a large flat-bottomed glass bowl. Arrange a single layer of the cake cubes in the bottom of the bowl. Spoon one-third of the macerated berries over the cake and then spread one-third of the mascarpone mixture over the berries. Repeat the layers twice, finishing with a layer of the mascarpone mixture. Cover with plastic wrap and refrigerate for at least 4 hours or for up to 24 hours to allow the flavors to marry.

Just before serving, garnish the trifle with whole berries and mint.

Serves 6

BON VOYAGE PARTY

When a friend or family member is about to embark on a trip, a travel-themed send-off lets the guests join in on the fun. The destination—Paris, in this case—sets the tone and inspires the decor, which includes French-style ceramics and flatware, as well as homemade place mats crafted from reproductions of vintage Parisian maps. Purple

hydrangeas and yellow and green accents give the room the feel of Paris in the spring. Guests are invited to bring small wrapped travel gifts, which are presented to the guest of honor in a colorful tote. A dry French rosé lends more color and pairs with the bright flavors of the menu.

TIPS FOR
CELEBRATORY DINNERS

- Think of the space as a stage to set a story relating to the occasion or to the guest of honor.

- Decorate the table with trinkets, maps, and tableware evoking the destination.

- Seat the guest of honor to the right of the host or in a central location.

- Adapt this party to other special occasions by substituting appropriate props and gifts.

MENU

Cherry Tomato and Fava Bean Salad

*North African Chicken Skewers
with Herbed Couscous*

Coconut Layer Cake

Dry French Rosé

WORK PLAN

AT LEAST ONE DAY IN ADVANCE

Make the preserved lemons for the skewers

Bake the cake and make the frosting

THE DAY OF THE PARTY

Shell the fava beans for the salad

Marinate the ingredients for the skewers

Assemble the cake

JUST BEFORE SERVING

Toss the salad ingredients

Broil the skewers and make the couscous

VINTAGE MAP PLACE MATS

Vintage maps can be easily fashioned into place mats that bring the guest of honor's destination right to the table. The mats become conversation pieces as guests hunt for locations and discuss the itinerary of the honoree.

gather the materials: reproductions of vintage maps (sometimes sold as gift wrap, or buy one original and make 11-by-17-inch color photocopies); a ruler; a pencil; pinking shears; and one of the dinner plates you will be using.

measure the first place mat by putting a plate on the center of the map. Allowing about 3 inches (7.5 cm) of visible map on all sides of the plate, mark cutting guidelines with a pencil.

trim the map along the pencil lines with pinking shears. Set it on the table with the plate to make sure it looks good before trimming the remaining mats to match.

CHERRY TOMATO AND FAVA BEAN SALAD

In this brightly colored first-course salad, fava beans are combined with pecorino romano, an Italian sheep's-milk cheese, and plump cherry tomatoes. Accompany with ready-made cheese crisps, thin toasted bread slices topped with cheese, available at specialty-food stores.

Remove the fava beans from their pods and discard the pods. (The beans can be shelled up to 8 hours in advance. Refrigerate until needed.)

Fill a large bowl three-fourths full of ice water and set aside. Bring a saucepan three-fourths full of water to a boil over high heat. Add the fava beans and boil until tender, 3–4 minutes. Drain the beans into a colander, then transfer them at once to the ice-water bath. When they are cool, drain them again into the colander. Using a thumb and forefinger, squeeze each bean from its tough skin into a small bowl, using a paring knife to make a tiny break in the skin at the edge of the bean first if necessary.

In a large bowl, toss together the fava beans, tomatoes, celery, and mint. Drizzle the olive oil and lemon juice over the top, season to taste with the salt and pepper, and toss again to coat.

Divide the salad evenly among individual plates. Using a vegetable peeler, shave the pecorino cheese evenly over the top. Garnish each serving with 2 cheese crisps, if using, and serve at once.

Serves 6

4 lb (2 kg) fava (broad) beans

2 cups (12 oz/375 g) cherry tomatoes in mixed colors and shapes, stems removed and cut in half

1 celery stalk, thinly sliced

12 fresh mint leaves, finely slivered

1/4 cup (2 fl oz/60 ml) extra-virgin olive oil

2 tablespoons fresh lemon juice

Coarse salt and freshly ground pepper

2-oz (60-g) wedge pecorino romano cheese

12 store-bought cheese crisps (see note; optional)

NORTH AFRICAN CHICKEN SKEWERS WITH HERBED COUSCOUS

QUICK PRESERVED LEMONS

4 large, thin-skinned organic lemons

6 cloves garlic, thinly sliced

1 teaspoon sugar

1 teaspoon coriander seeds, crushed

Coarse salt

2/3 cup (5 fl oz/160 ml) fresh lemon juice

2 tablespoons olive oil

CHICKEN SKEWERS

1 teaspoon *each* ground cumin, ground turmeric, and ground cinnamon

1 teaspoon mild Spanish smoked paprika, *pimentón de La Vera*

1/2 teaspoon saffron threads

1 clove garlic, minced

1/2 cup (1/2 oz/15 g) fresh cilantro (fresh coriander) leaves, chopped

1/3 cup (2 oz/60 g) almonds, coarsely chopped

3 tablespoons olive oil

3 lb (1.5 kg) boneless, skinless chicken breasts, cut into 1¹/2-inch (4-cm) cubes

32 extra-large green olives, pitted

HERBED COUSCOUS

2 cups (12 oz/375 g) instant couscous

2 cups (16 fl oz/500 ml) boiling water

3 tablespoons unsalted butter, at room temperature

1/2 cup (3/4 oz/20 g) chopped mixed fresh herbs of choice

Coarse salt and freshly ground pepper

Paprika for sprinkling

Inspired by a classic Moroccan dish in which chicken is simmered with preserved lemons and green olives, these brochettes are surprisingly simple to make. An easy side dish of steamed couscous with fresh herbs is a fitting companion.

To make the preserved lemons, preheat the oven to 400°F (200°C). Cut a thin slice off both ends of each lemon. Cut each lemon into 8 wedges, and place the wedges in a nonreactive baking dish just large enough to hold them in a single layer. Add the garlic, sugar, coriander seeds, 3 tablespoons salt, the lemon juice, and olive oil and toss to coat evenly. Cover the dish loosely with aluminum foil. Bake the lemon wedges for 10 minutes, then turn off the oven and leave them in the oven overnight. In the morning, transfer the contents of the dish to an airtight container and refrigerate until ready to use; they will keep for up to 2 weeks.

To make the skewers, in a shallow glass bowl, stir together the cumin, turmeric, cinnamon, paprika, saffron, garlic, cilantro, almonds, and olive oil until well mixed. Add the chicken, olives, and 16 of the lemon wedges (reserve the rest for another use) and toss to coat with the spice mixture. Cover and refrigerate for 4–8 hours.

Preheat the broiler (grill). Have ready 8 metal skewers. Remove the chicken, olives, and lemon wedges from the marinade; discard the marinade. Thread the ingredients onto each skewer, arranging them in your desired pattern and dividing them evenly. Do not crowd the pieces too tightly, or the chicken will not cook evenly. Place the skewers on a rimmed baking sheet and place under the broiler about 6 inches (15 cm) from the heat source. Broil (grill) until lightly browned, about 5 minutes. Turn the skewers and continue to broil until the chicken is golden and opaque throughout, about 5 minutes longer.

Meanwhile, make the couscous: Put the couscous in a heatproof bowl. Add the boiling water, cover, and let stand until absorbed, about 5 minutes. Fluff the couscous with a fork, then stir in the butter and herbs. Season with salt and pepper.

Divide the couscous among warmed individual plates and sprinkle with paprika. Slide the contents off the skewers onto each plate, dividing evenly. Serve at once.

Serves 6

COCONUT LAYER CAKE

This luscious dessert is for anyone who likes coconut: coconut-flavored cake layers are topped with a light and fluffy coconut frosting. A generous amount of shredded coconut is then showered over the top.

Preheat the oven to 350°F (180°C). Line the bottom of a straight-sided 9-by-13-inch (23-by-33-cm) pan with parchment (baking) paper. Lightly butter the parchment and the sides of the pan. Dust with flour, and tap out the excess.

In a bowl, sift together the flour, baking powder, and salt. In a separate bowl, stir together the milk and coconut and vanilla extracts. In a large bowl, using a mixer on medium-high speed, beat together the butter and granulated sugar until fluffy, about 5 minutes. Add the eggs one at a time, beating well after each addition. Reduce the speed to low. Add the flour mixture in 3 batches alternately with the milk mixture, beginning and ending with the flour mixture and stopping to scrape down the sides of the bowl as needed. Using a rubber spatula, fold in the coconut.

Pour the batter into the prepared pan. Bake the cake until the top is golden and a toothpick inserted into the center comes out clean, about 40 minutes. Transfer to a wire rack and let the cake cool completely in the pan, about 1 hour. (The cake can be baked the night before serving, loosely covered, and refrigerated.)

Meanwhile, make the frosting: In a bowl, using the mixer on medium-high speed, whip together the cream and ¹/₂ cup (2 oz/60 g) of the confectioners' sugar until stiff peaks form, about 2 minutes. In a separate bowl, beat together the cream cheese and the remaining ¹/₂ cup confectioners' sugar until light and fluffy, about 5 minutes. Using a rubber spatula, fold the cream cheese mixture into the whipped cream. Fold in the coconut extract. Cover and refrigerate until needed.

To assemble, run a knife blade around the inside edge of the pan to loosen the cake, then invert it onto a work surface. Lift off the pan and parchment. Cut the cake in half lengthwise. Transfer one-half to a serving platter. Spread one-third of the frosting over the top and sprinkle with one-third of the coconut. Carefully place the second rectangle on top of the first. Spread the remaining frosting over the top and sides of the cake. Press the remaining two-thirds of the coconut evenly over the top and sides of the cake, covering completely. Cut into thick slices to serve.

Serves 6

2¹/₂ cups (10 oz/315 g) cake (soft-wheat) flour

2 teaspoons baking powder

¹/₄ teaspoon salt

1 cup (8 fl oz/250 ml) whole milk

1 teaspoon coconut extract (essence)

1 teaspoon vanilla extract (essence)

1 cup (8 oz/250 g) unsalted butter, at room temperature

1¹/₂ cups (12 oz/375 g) granulated sugar

4 large eggs

¹/₂ cup (2 oz/60 g) sweetened shredded dried coconut

COCONUT FROSTING

2 cups (16 fl oz/500 ml) heavy (double) cream

1 cup (4 oz/120 g) confectioners' (icing) sugar

¹/₂ lb (250 g) cream cheese, at room temperature

¹/₄ teaspoon coconut extract (essence)

3 cups (12 oz/375 g) sweetened shredded dried coconut

SUMMER

MENUS FOR SUMMER

SOLSTICE DINNER

Blended Mojitos

Shrimp Ceviche in Cucumber Cups

Scallop, Mango, and Avocado Salad

Seared Beef Tenderloin with Cilantro and Mint

Brown Sugar Peaches with Ice Cream

88

GARDEN PARTY

Kir Royales

Herbed Gougères

Chilled Two-Pea Soup with Mint

Broiled Sea Bass with Summer Vegetables and Saffron Jus

Summer Greens with Lemon Vinaigrette

Warm Fruit Galettes

106

SUMMER BARBECUE

Watermelon Agua Fresca

Celery Slaw with Shrimp

Fire-Roasted Corn Salad

Grilled Potato Salad

Lemon-Herb Chicken Breasts

Chipotle Baby Back Ribs

Berry Cobbler

126

SEASIDE SUPPER

Summer Vegetable Gazpacho

Garlic Toasts

Spanish-Style Steamed Shellfish

Flan with Fresh Figs

146

SOLSTICE DINNER

On a warm summer evening in the city, a deck, patio, or rooftop can be a magical setting for a no-dining-table dinner party. As the sun sets and the cityscape below begins to sparkle, the setting is illuminated by decorative lights strung along the railing and deep-seated, oversized candles, which won't tumble and won't blow out.

Frosty blended mojitos set the Caribbean-cool mood of the meal to come. Suffused with the tropical flavors of lime and spices, the refreshing menu requires little cooking and heating, making it ideal for warm-weather entertaining.

MENU

Blended Mojitos

Shrimp Ceviche in Cucumber Cups

Scallop, Mango, and Avocado Salad

*Seared Beef Tenderloin with
Cilantro and Mint*

*Brown Sugar Peaches with
Ice Cream*

Pinot Gris

TIPS FOR PATIO DINING

- Set out pots of fresh basil or citronella candles to help keep insects at bay.

- Choose recipes that can be eaten at room temperature, and will not be affected by a breeze.

- Serve food that does not need a knife so guests can eat on their laps.

- Check outdoor furniture to make sure it is clean and comfortable; if needed, provide cushions.

- Offer bowls of nuts for snacking while sipping cocktails.

WORK PLAN

AT LEAST ONE DAY IN ADVANCE
Cut the cucumber cups for the ceviche

Make the balsamic syrup for the tenderloin

THE DAY OF THE PARTY
Marinate the ceviche

Make the vinaigrette for the salad

Sear the tenderloin

JUST BEFORE SERVING
Spoon the ceviche into the cucumber cups

Prepare the salad

Slice the seared tenderloin

Sauté the peaches

TROPICAL DRINK HOLDERS

Frozen drinks are refreshing, but they can be uncomfortable to hold for long periods of time. These decorative leaf-wrapped glasses protect guests' hands from the cold—and add a bit of island style to match the menu.

organize the supplies you'll need: flax leaves and raffia, available from florists and floral-supply wholesalers; tall glasses with smooth, straight sides; tape; and scissors.

wrap a single flax leaf at a slight angle around each glass, starting at the base and overlapping the layers tightly. Secure the end of the leaf temporarily with tape.

tie a long strip of raffia around the glass, securing it with a bow or neat knot to hold the leaf in place. Trim the end of the raffia, as needed, and remove the tape.

run a lime wedge around the rim of a glass to moisten it. Repeat with the remaining glasses.

pour the blended drinks into the prepared glasses in a steady stream, taking care not to disturb the sugared rims.

dip the moistened rim of each glass into a plate or shallow bowl filled with sugar. Place in the freezer to chill.

garnish each glass with a mint sprig and a lime wedge skewered on a natural bamboo cocktail pick.

BLENDED MOJITOS

A refreshing drink of lime, mint, and rum, the mojito is the perfect cocktail for a summer evening. Here, it is blended, margarita style, and served in a tall glass with a sugared rim.

12 fresh mint sprigs, each about 8 inches (20 cm) long, plus 1/2 cup (1/2 oz/15 g) fresh leaves

1/2 cup (4 oz/125 g) sugar

1/2 cup (4 fl oz/125 ml) fresh lime juice

1 cup (8 fl oz/250 ml) light rum

Sugar and 1 or 2 lime wedges for coating rims

Ice cubes

2 cups (16 fl oz/500 ml) club soda

GARNISHES

1 lime, cut into 4 wedges

4 small fresh mint sprigs

In a medium bowl, using the back of a wooden spoon, crush together the mint sprigs, sugar, and lime juice. Pour in the rum, cover with plastic wrap, and let stand at room temperature for at least 2 hours or for up to overnight.

Select 4 tall, slender glasses. Spread a layer of sugar on a small, flat plate. Working with 1 glass at a time, run a lime wedge around the edge of the glass to moisten it, then dip the rim into the sugar to coat it evenly. Put the glasses in the freezer to chill for at least 15 minutes.

When ready to make the mojitos, fill a blender halfway with ice cubes. Pour the rum mixture through a fine-mesh sieve into the blender. Add the club soda and the 1/2 cup mint leaves and purée until well blended.

Divide the mixture evenly among the chilled glasses. Garnish each glass with a lime wedge and a mint sprig.

Serves 4

SHRIMP CEVICHE IN CUCUMBER CUPS

Perfectly fresh seafood is essential when preparing ceviche. Buy only shrimp displayed on ice and labeled "fresh," rather than "previously frozen." It is always worth asking the fishmonger if you are uncertain. If desired, arrange the filled cups on a platter lined with ti leaves.

Peel the cucumbers, then cut them into slices $^5/_8$ inch (1.5 cm) thick. You should have 16 slices total.

Using a fluted cookie cutter $1^1/_2$ inches (4 cm) in diameter, cut each cucumber slice to create a slice with fluted edges. Using a melon baller, scoop out a little of the center of each slice to form a well, being careful not to pierce the bottom. Transfer the cucumber cups to a baking sheet lined with paper towels, cover with plastic wrap, and refrigerate until serving. (The cucumber cups can be prepared up to 1 day in advance.)

In a nonreactive bowl, combine the shrimp, lime juice, red onion, cilantro, snipped chives, red and yellow bell peppers, ginger, cumin, a pinch of cayenne pepper, 1 teaspoon salt, and $^1/_2$ teaspoon black pepper. Stir to mix, cover, and refrigerate for at least 2 hours or for up to 4 hours, stirring from time to time.

Just before serving, transfer the shrimp mixture to a fine-mesh sieve placed over a bowl to drain off all the liquid. Discard the liquid. Return the shrimp mixture to its original bowl and stir in the sour cream. Fill each cucumber cup with an equal amount of the ceviche.

Garnish each cup with 2 chive pieces and sprinkle with paprika. Arrange on a chilled platter and serve at once.

Serves 4

2 English (hothouse) cucumbers, each about $1^3/_4$ inches (4.5 cm) in diameter

$^1/_2$ lb (250 g) shrimp (prawns), peeled, deveined, and finely chopped

Juice of 4 limes

2 tablespoons minced red onion

2 tablespoons chopped fresh cilantro (fresh coriander)

1 tablespoon snipped fresh chives, plus 32 pieces fresh chive, each 1 inch (2.5 cm) long

2 tablespoons minced red bell pepper (capsicum)

2 tablespoons minced yellow bell pepper (capsicum)

2 teaspoons peeled and grated fresh ginger

1 teaspoon ground cumin

Cayenne pepper

Coarse salt and freshly ground black pepper

2 tablespoons sour cream

Paprika for sprinkling

Scallop, Mango, and Avocado Salad

Look for uniformly sized sea scallops about 1½ inches (4 cm) in diameter. They should be pale ivory or have the lightest hint of pink, with a mild, sweet scent. The combination of scallops, mango, and avocado results in a particularly rich salad. For a lighter course, omit the scallops.

CHILE-LIME VINAIGRETTE

½ jalapeño chile, seeded and minced

Juice of 2 limes

¼ cup (2 fl oz/60 ml) olive oil

Coarse salt and freshly ground pepper

1 mango

1 avocado, halved, pitted, peeled, and cut into ½-inch (12-mm) cubes

Juice of ½ lime

2 tablespoons unsalted butter, melted

12 sea scallops

Coarse salt and freshly ground pepper

6 cups (6 oz/185 g) mixed salad greens

2 green (spring) onions, including tender green tops, sliced on the diagonal

To make the vinaigrette, in a small bowl, combine the jalapeño and lime juice. Whisk in the olive oil. Season with ½ teaspoon salt and pepper to taste. Set aside until serving. (The vinaigrette can be made up to 2 hours in advance.)

Stand the mango on one of its narrow sides on a cutting board. Using a sharp knife, cut slightly off center, slicing off all the flesh from one side of the pit in a single piece. Repeat on the other side of the pit. Hold 1 section, flesh side up, in your hand. With the tip of the knife, score the flesh lengthwise and then crosswise, forming ½-inch (12-mm) cubes and taking care not to cut through the peel. Press against the center of the peel to force the cubes upward, then run the knife along the base of the cubes to free them, allowing them to drop into a nonreactive bowl. Repeat with the remaining section. Add the avocado and lime juice to the mango cubes and toss together. Set aside.

Preheat the broiler (grill). Line a rimmed baking sheet with aluminum foil. Put the melted butter in a shallow bowl. Add the scallops and turn to coat lightly. Arrange the scallops on the baking sheet, spacing them evenly. Season with salt and pepper. Slip the scallops under the broiler about 6 inches (15 cm) from the heat source and broil (grill) until golden on top, about 1½ minutes. Turn the scallops over and broil until the tops are golden and the centers are nearly translucent, about 1 minute longer. Remove from the broiler.

In a bowl, toss the salad greens with half of the vinaigrette and divide them among chilled individual plates. Divide the mango and avocado cubes evenly among the salad greens, scattering them on top. Place 3 scallops on each salad. Add any pan juices from the scallops to the remaining vinaigrette, stir to mix, and then drizzle the vinaigrette on and around the scallops. Garnish the salad portions with the green onions and serve at once.

Serves 4

Seared Beef Tenderloin with Cilantro and Mint

For this recipe, beef tenderloin is well seasoned, quickly seared, and then sliced paper-thin, a simple preparation that preserves the cut's natural tenderness. If you prefer your tenderloin more fully cooked, increase the cooking time to 8 to 10 minutes.

To make the balsamic syrup, pour the vinegar into a small saucepan, place over low heat, bring to a gentle simmer, and cook until reduced to ½ cup (4 fl oz/ 125 ml), about 1½ hours. The vinegar will have become syrupy. Remove from the heat and let cool to room temperature. Transfer the syrup to a small bowl, cover, and refrigerate until needed. Set aside 2 tablespoons for this recipe; reserve the remainder for another use. (The balsamic syrup will keep, tightly capped, for up to 1 month.)

Remove the beef from the refrigerator about 30 minutes before you plan to cook it.

In a small bowl, stir together the ginger, garlic and onion powders, cumin and coriander seeds, cilantro, and 1 teaspoon each salt and pepper. Spread the mixture on a large flat plate. Brush the beef fillet on all sides with the mustard. Roll the fillet in the spice mixture, coating it evenly and pressing the mixture lightly with your fingers so that it adheres to the surface.

In a large, nonstick frying pan over high heat, warm the olive oil. When the oil is hot, add the fillet and sear, turning as needed, until browned evenly on all sides, about 5 minutes; the meat will still be rare in the center. Let the meat rest for about 10 minutes. (The meat can be done up to this point 1 hour in advance.) Transfer to a cutting board and slice against the grain as thinly as possible.

Divide the slices evenly among individual plates, folding the pieces and overlapping them slightly to cover the center of each plate. Scatter the cilantro, mint, and green onions over the beef slices. Finish each plate with a drizzle of extra-virgin olive oil and the reserved balsamic syrup. Serve at once.

Serves 4

BALSAMIC SYRUP

2 cups (16 fl oz/500 ml) young balsamic vinegar

1½-lb (750-g) piece of beef tenderloin, trimmed

1 teaspoon ground ginger

1 teaspoon garlic powder

1 teaspoon onion powder

1 teaspoon cumin seeds, crushed

1 teaspoon coriander seeds, crushed

2 tablespoons chopped fresh cilantro (fresh coriander)

Coarse salt and freshly ground pepper

1 tablespoon Dijon mustard

2 tablespoons olive oil

GARNISHES

⅓ cup (⅓ oz/10 g) fresh cilantro (fresh coriander) leaves, torn into pieces

6 fresh mint leaves, finely slivered

2 green (spring) onions, including tender green tops, thinly sliced on the diagonal

2 tablespoons fruity extra-virgin olive oil

Brown Sugar Peaches with Ice Cream

Summertime's sweet, fragrant stone fruits are wonderful for making quick and easy desserts. Here, a scoop of ice cream is topped with warm, lightly sugared peach slices. Look for deep yellow peaches that give slightly to gentle pressure, signs that they are juicy and flavorful.

4 peaches

Juice of $1/2$ lemon

4 tablespoons (2 oz/60 g) unsalted butter

$1/4$ cup (2 oz/60 g) firmly packed golden brown sugar

2 tablespoons dark rum (optional)

1 pt (16 fl oz/500 ml) rum raisin, vanilla, or coffee ice cream

If desired, rub off any excess peach fuzz with a kitchen towel. Halve and pit the peaches, then cut them into slices $1/2$ inch (12 mm) thick.

In a nonreactive bowl, toss together the peach slices and lemon juice. Set aside.

In a large frying pan over medium heat, melt the butter. Add the peaches and brown sugar and sauté the peaches until they are lightly browned and the sugar has caramelized, about 5 minutes. Remove from the heat and swirl in the rum, if using.

To serve, scoop the ice cream into martini glasses or individual bowls. Top each serving with an equal amount of the warm peaches and drizzle with an equal amount of the pan juices. Serve at once.

Serves 4

GARDEN PARTY

Guests delight in the warmth of a summer afternoon in a splendid outdoor dining room. All the elements of an elegant party are here: the crisp, white tablecloth; the gleam of special-occasion flatware, plates, glasses, and silver place-card holders. But when they are re-set in the garden amid flowers and dappled shade, their formality is transformed into comfortable country charm.

Peonies, garden roses, and lavender are gathered from the yard and arranged on the table in silver cups, and votive candles are set out for when the sunlight fades. The menu makes the most of the season's best fresh ingredients.

WORK PLAN

AT LEAST ONE DAY IN ADVANCE

Make the dough for the galettes

Make the soup

THE DAY OF THE PARTY

Bake the *gougères*

Make the vinaigrette and toast the walnuts for the salad

Prepare the lavender crème fraîche

JUST BEFORE SERVING

Reheat the *gougères*

Assemble the salad

Make the sea bass dish

Bake the galettes

MENU

Kir Royales

Herbed Gougères

Chilled Two-Pea Soup with Mint

*Broiled Sea Bass with Summer
Vegetables and Saffron Jus*

Summer Greens with Lemon Vinaigrette

Warm Fruit Galettes

White Burgundy

TIPS FOR ELEGANT
OUTDOOR DINING

- The day before, watch the path of the
  sun to find a spot for the table with
  the right mix of shade and sun.

- Position the table close to the kitchen
  for ease in serving.

- Serve cocktails and hors d'oeuvres in
  another part of the garden.

- If using candles as part of the table
  decoration, wait to light them until
  the sun begins to set.

DECORATIVE NAPKIN FOLD

Bring a decorative touch to each place setting by repeating the appearance of a flower or herb sprig from the centerpiece. This simple napkin fold creates a pocket for that purpose.

place a large napkin, folded in quarters with open points at the top, on a work surface. Fold down the top two layers, matching up the points.

fold the bottom point of the napkin up so that it covers the left and right points. Turn the napkin over; its shape should resemble a bishop's hat.

flip the napkin over, smooth out the edges, then fold the left and right sides in. The points should meet at the center of the napkin.

tuck sprigs of lavender, tied together with decorative ribbon, into the pocket of each napkin. Place the napkin on top of the plate at each place setting.

open a chilled bottle of Champagne or other sparkling wine, following the directions on page 302.

drizzle a small amount of *crème de cassis* into each chilled Champagne flute. The more liqueur you use, the sweeter and darker the drink will be.

fill each glass with Champagne, pouring the wine in a slow, steady stream down the side of the glass to keep it from foaming and bubbling over the top.

KIR ROYALES

For best results, look for a high-quality crème de cassis *(black currant liqueur)—the best come from the Dijon region of France—for these refreshing Burgundian-style cocktails.*

About 1/3 cup (3 fl oz/80 ml) *crème de cassis*

2 bottles (24 fl oz/750 ml each) Champagne or other sparkling wine, well chilled

Put 8 Champagne flutes in the freezer to chill for at least 15 minutes. Pour 1–2 teaspoons *crème de cassis* into each chilled flute (more *cassis* will yield a sweeter cocktail). Slowly fill the flutes with Champagne. Serve at once.

Serves 8

HERBED GOUGÈRES

In this simple French-inspired recipe, gougères, *classic cheese puffs from Burgundy, are laden with fresh herbs. As you welcome your guests into the garden, pass the puffs along with small linen napkins and a cocktail.*

Position 2 oven racks near the center of the oven and preheat to 400°F (200°C). Line 2 rimmed baking sheets with parchment (baking) paper.

Sift the flour onto another sheet of parchment and set aside. Pour the water into a deep saucepan and add the butter and a pinch of salt. Bring to a boil over high heat, stirring to ensure that the butter melts completely before the water reaches a boil. Reduce the heat to medium and add the reserved flour all at once while stirring briskly with a wooden spatula. Continue stirring until the flour rolls off the walls of the saucepan and clings in a ball to the spatula, 30–40 seconds, evaporating as much water as possible without scorching the pastry. Remove from the heat. Transfer the pastry to a bowl and let cool for 3 minutes. Add the eggs one at a time, stirring well after each addition.

Using the spatula, fold the Gruyère cheese, ⅓ cup herbs, garlic, ½ teaspoon salt, and ¼ teaspoon pepper into the pastry. Have ready a glass or bowl of cold water. Dip a small ice-cream scoop—1¼ inches (3 cm) in diameter—into the water, use it to scoop up a portion of the pastry, and then release the ball onto a prepared baking sheet. Repeat with the remaining pastry, moistening the scoop each time and spacing the balls about 2 inches (5 cm) apart on the baking sheets.

Bake the puffs until golden brown, about 20 minutes, switching the baking sheets between the racks and rotating them 180 degrees at the midway point. Turn off the oven, open the oven door, and let the puffs air-dry for 5–10 minutes. This ensures that they will be crispy. Remove the baking sheets from the oven and tap each sheet gently on a countertop to release the baked puffs from the parchment. (The cooled puffs can be stored at room temperature in an airtight container for up to 4 hours before serving. Reheat them on a baking sheet in a single layer at 300°F/150°C until heated through, about 10 minutes.)

Transfer the hot puffs to a serving platter, sprinkle with the additional herbs, and serve at once.

Serves 8

1 cup (5 oz/155 g) all-purpose (plain) flour

1 cup (8 fl oz/250 ml) water

5 tablespoons (2½ oz/75 g) unsalted butter, cut into small cubes

Coarse salt

4 large eggs

3 tablespoons finely diced Gruyère cheese

⅓ cup (½ oz/15 g) chopped fresh chervil, rosemary, and chives, in equal parts, plus more for garnish

1 clove garlic, finely chopped

Freshly ground pepper

CHILLED TWO-PEA SOUP WITH MINT

Two pea varieties, sweet English and brightly flavored sugar snap, star in this light puréed soup. Fresh mint is a natural partner, lending its clean flavor. Including at least one cold dish on a party menu is a good idea, as it frees you to make sure other dishes are piping hot at serving time.

In a large saucepan over medium heat, warm the canola oil. Add the green onions and sauté, stirring occasionally, until softened, 3–5 minutes. Add the lettuce and sauté until soft, about 5 minutes.

Add the mint, broth, sugar snap peas, and English peas to the saucepan and mix well. Reduce the heat to low, cover, and simmer until the peas are tender, about 20 minutes. Remove from the heat and let cool slightly.

Working in batches, in a blender or food processor, process the soup until a smooth purée forms. Return the purée to the pan, add the lemon juice, and season to taste with salt and white pepper. Return the pan to medium heat, bring to a simmer, and cook for about 3 minutes to blend the flavors.

Remove the soup from the heat and pour it into a glass pitcher or bowl. Let the soup cool to room temperature, then cover and refrigerate until well chilled, at least 4 hours or for up to 24 hours. Chill soup bowls at the same time.

Taste and adjust the seasoning again just before serving. Pour or ladle the soup into the chilled soup bowls. Garnish each serving with an equal amount of the crème fraîche and chives.

Serves 8

2 tablespoons canola oil

6 green (spring) onions, white parts only, finely chopped

1 head butter (Boston) lettuce, cored and shredded

3 tablespoons coarsely chopped fresh mint

4 cups (32 fl oz/1 l) reduced-sodium chicken broth

1/2 lb (250 g) sugar snap peas, trimmed

1 cup (5 oz/155 g) shelled English peas or thawed frozen petite peas

1 tablespoon fresh lemon juice

Coarse salt and freshly ground white pepper

1/4 cup (2 oz/60 g) crème fraîche or sour cream

Snipped fresh chives for garnish

Broiled Sea Bass with Summer Vegetables and Saffron Jus

Some of summertime's most prized vegetables form a bed for lightly seasoned sea bass fillets. An easy sauce of saffron, white wine, and crème fraîche complements the ingredients.

In a small bowl, combine the saffron and wine and set aside for 10 minutes. In a saucepan over medium heat, melt the 2 tablespoons butter. Add the shallots and sauté until soft, about 2 minutes. Stir in the saffron-wine mixture and the broth and bring to a simmer. Cook until reduced by half, about 10 minutes. Remove from the heat, whisk in the crème fraîche, and season to taste with salt and pepper. Keep warm.

Have ready a large bowl of water to which you have added the lemon juice. Working with 1 artichoke at a time, pull off and discard the tough outer leaves until you reach the pale green inner leaves. Cut the stem off flush with the bottom and discard it. Slice off the top one-third to one-half of the leaves, then cut the artichoke lengthwise into sixths. If an inedible fuzzy choke has begun to form, cut it out of each piece, then drop the pieces into the lemon water.

Bring a large saucepan three-fourths full of salted water to a boil, add the haricots verts, and parboil for 1 1/2 minutes, then drain and refresh under running cold water. Set aside. In a large frying pan over medium heat, warm the olive oil. Drain the artichokes and add to the pan along with the fennel. Sauté until the vegetables are lightly golden and just tender, about 6 minutes. Add the haricots verts and cook until they are warmed through, about 2 minutes. Add the parsley and chives, toss to mix, and season with salt and pepper. Remove from the heat and keep warm.

Preheat the broiler (grill). Place the fish fillets, skin side down, on a rimmed baking sheet and brush with the melted butter. Sprinkle the fennel seeds and 1/2 teaspoon each salt and pepper evenly over the top. Place under the broiler about 7 inches (18 cm) from the heat source and broil (grill), without turning, until crisp on the top and just opaque at the center when tested with a knife, 5–6 minutes.

Divide the vegetables evenly among warmed individual plates. Top each serving with a piece of fish, and spoon the saffron *jus* evenly over the top. Garnish with the reserved fennel fronds and serve at once.

Serves 8

1 teaspoon saffron threads, crushed

1 cup (8 fl oz/250 ml) dry white wine

2 tablespoons unsalted butter, plus 4 tablespoons (2 oz/60 g) unsalted butter, melted

2 shallots, chopped

2 cups (16 fl oz/500 ml) reduced-sodium chicken broth

1/2 cup (4 oz/125 g) crème fraîche

Coarse salt and freshly ground pepper

Juice of 1 lemon

16 small artichokes

1/2 lb (250 g) haricots verts, trimmed

1/3 cup (3 fl oz/80 ml) olive oil

2 or 3 fennel bulbs, trimmed, cored, and thinly sliced lengthwise, plus fronds reserved for garnish

2 tablespoons chopped fresh flat-leaf (Italian) parsley

2 tablespoons snipped fresh chives

8 sea bass fillets with skin intact, each 6 oz (185 g) and about 1 1/2 inches (4 cm) thick

2 tablespoons fennel seeds, crushed

SUMMER GREENS WITH LEMON VINAIGRETTE

Look for impeccably fresh greens for this seasonal salad. Yellow-tipped Belgian endive is more readily available and can be used on its own if you cannot find the red-tipped variety. Store the endives in a paper bag in the refrigerator, as they will become bitter if exposed to light.

LEMON VINAIGRETTE

2^1/$_2$ tablespoons extra-virgin olive oil

1 tablespoon fresh lemon juice

1 small shallot, minced

Coarse salt and freshly ground pepper

^{1}/$_2$ cup (2 oz/60 g) walnut pieces

2 heads yellow-tipped Belgian endive (chicory/witloof), cored and cut lengthwise into narrow strips

2 heads red-tipped Belgian endive (chicory/witloof), cored and cut lengthwise into narrow strips

2 bunches young, tender watercress, tough stems removed

To make the vinaigrette, in a small bowl, whisk together the olive oil, lemon juice, and shallot. Season to taste with salt and pepper. Let stand for 30 minutes or for up to 4 hours to blend the flavors.

In a small, dry frying pan over medium heat, toast the nuts, shaking the pan often, until they start to brown and smell aromatic, about 7 minutes. Transfer to a small dish and set aside.

In a large bowl, combine the endives and watercress. Whisk the vinaigrette, drizzle it over the greens, and toss to coat the leaves well. Divide the salad evenly among individual plates and top with the toasted walnuts. Serve at once.

Serves 8

Warm Fruit Galettes

These rustic free-form galettes are served warm from the oven topped with an easy sauce made by stirring dried lavender into crème fraîche. For the best flavor, choose fruits at the peak of ripeness. You can also use peaches in place of the plums, and raspberries can stand in for the blackberries.

To make the dough, in a food processor, combine the flour and salt and pulse briefly to mix. Add the butter and shortening and pulse until the pieces are the size of large peas. Drizzle in the ice water and pulse just until the dough begins to come together. Transfer to a work surface. Gather the dough into a ball, divide it into 8 equal portions, flatten each portion into a disk, and wrap each disk in plastic wrap. Refrigerate for at least 2 hours or for up to 24 hours.

Position 2 racks near the center of the oven and preheat to 425°F (220°C). Line 2 rimmed baking sheets with parchment (baking) paper. Unwrap the dough disks, place on a lightly floured work surface, and let rest for 10–15 minutes.

Roll out a dough disk into a round roughly 8 inches (20 cm) in diameter and ¹/₈ inch (3 mm) thick. Starting 1¹/₂ inches (4 cm) in from the edge of the disk, arrange one-eighth of the plum slices on top, creating concentric circles and overlapping the slices slightly. Scatter ¹/₂ cup (2 oz/60 g) of the berries over the top and sprinkle with ³/₄ teaspoon of the granulated sugar. Fold the uncovered 1¹/₂-inch edge of the dough up over the fruit to make a broad rim. Repeat with the remaining dough disks, fruit, and granulated sugar. As each galette is formed, transfer it to a prepared baking sheet.

Brush the rims of the crusts with the egg-water mixture, then sprinkle evenly with the coarse sugar. Bake the galettes until the crusts are golden brown and the fruit is tender when pierced with a knife, about 40 minutes, switching the baking sheets between the racks and rotating them 180 degrees at the midway point.

To make the lavender crème fraîche, in a small bowl, stir together the crème fraîche, lavender, and granulated sugar to taste, if using. Cover and refrigerate until needed.

When the galettes are ready, remove from the oven and let cool slightly on the baking sheets on wire racks. Divide the galettes among individual plates. Serve at once, each with a large spoonful of the crème fraîche.

Serves 8

PASTRY DOUGH

4 cups (1¹/₄ lb/625 g) unbleached all-purpose (plain) flour

1¹/₂ teaspoons salt

1 cup (8 oz/250 g) chilled unsalted butter, cut into small pieces

³/₄ cup (6 oz/185 g) plus 2 tablespoons chilled solid vegetable shortening, cut into small pieces

¹/₂ cup (4 fl oz/125 ml) ice water

1 lb (500 g) yellow and/or purple plums, halved, pitted, and thinly sliced

4 cups (1 lb/500 g) blackberries

2 tablespoons granulated sugar

1 egg yolk whisked with 1 teaspoon water

2 tablespoons coarse sugar

LAVENDER CRÈME FRAÎCHE

1 cup (8 oz/250 g) crème fraîche

1 tablespoon fresh lavender flowers, crushed

Granulated sugar (optional)

SUMMER BARBECUE

The backyard barbecue is a time-honored American custom, but a few special touches are all it takes to turn it into a stylish and memorable occasion. The weathered wooden table is set with real dishes, glasses, and cutlery, instead of plastic or paper ware, and brightly colored red, white, and blue bandannas stand in for napkins.

Homemade party favors—canning jars filled with summer preserves, pickles, or barbecue sauce—do double duty as decorative place cards. The menu, updates of summer classics served family style on large platters, is designed to be prepared in stages, firing up the grill just once.

MENU

Watermelon Agua Fresca

Celery Slaw with Shrimp

Fire-Roasted Corn Salad

Grilled Potato Salad

Lemon-Herb Chicken Breasts

Chipotle Baby Back Ribs

Berry Cobbler

TIPS FOR BARBECUES

- Fill a large galvanized bucket with ice and pack it with beer, bottled water, and sodas.

- Freeze strips of citrus peel in ice cubes to flavor cold drinks.

- Use small galvanized metal containers, first lined with plastic, to hold chips or fresh berries for snacking.

- Serve this menu for any summer holiday, such as the Fourth of July or Labor Day.

WORK PLAN

AT LEAST ONE DAY IN ADVANCE

Make the vinaigrette for the slaw

Purée the dressing and parboil the
potatoes for the potato salad

Coat the ribs with the spice paste

THE DAY OF THE PARTY

Cut the vegetables and fry the
bacon for the slaw

Marinate the chicken

Roast the ribs (the first phase of cooking)

Bake the cobbler

JUST BEFORE SERVING

Grill the corn, potatoes, chicken, and ribs

Put together the slaw

Assemble the corn and potato salads

CANNING JAR
PARTY FAVORS

Small, attractive canning jars filled with homemade preserves, pickled peppers, or some of the barbecue sauce you made for the ribs are edible party souvenirs for your guests to take home. Decorative labels personalize each jar and also serve as place cards.

assemble the supplies you will need: small filled canning jars, bright-colored bandannas, rubber bands, ribbon, scissors, decorative labels, and a pen.

tie a length of ribbon around the neck of each jar, hiding the rubber band. Trim the ends of the ribbon for a finished look.

trim the bandannas into squares 3 to 4 inches larger than the diameter of the jar lids. Place a square over each lid and secure it with a rubber band.

label each jar, indicating its contents and the name of the recipient. Put a jar at each place setting.

purée seedless watermelon pulp in batches, transferring each batch to a large mixing bowl or pitcher. Add lime juice, sugar, and mint and let steep for 1 to 3 hours.

strain the purée through a medium-mesh sieve into a widemouthed jar—like you might see in a Mexican restaurant—or pitcher.

fill the jar with ice cubes, lime slices, and sparkling water. Provide a ladle for serving, if needed, and garnish each drink with a fresh mint sprig.

WATERMELON AGUA FRESCA

Mexican agua fresca, lightly sweetened, crushed fresh fruit stirred together with a little water, is a refreshing alternative to iced tea or lemonade. Mix all the ingredients in a large, widemouthed jar and set out a ladle alongside, then let guests serve themselves.

1 very ripe, red seedless watermelon, about 12 lb (6 kg)

Juice of 4 limes

3/4 cup (6 oz/185 g) sugar

1 cup (1 oz/30 g) crushed fresh mint leaves, plus sprigs for garnish

4 cups (32 fl oz/1 l) sparkling water

3 limes, thinly sliced

2 qt (2 l) ice cubes

Cut the watermelon in half and, using a metal spoon, scoop out the flesh into a large bowl. Working in batches, purée the watermelon in a blender or food processor. As each batch is ready, transfer it to another large bowl. Add the lime juice, sugar, and mint leaves to the purée and stir to dissolve the sugar and combine the ingredients. Cover and set aside at room temperature for at least 1 hour or for up to 3 hours to allow the flavors to develop.

Pour the watermelon mixture through a medium-mesh sieve into a large, clear glass jar. Add the sparkling water, lime slices, and ice. Ladle or pour into glasses and garnish each glass with a mint sprig.

Serves 8

CELERY SLAW WITH SHRIMP

Old-fashioned coleslaw is updated here with generous additions of celery, radishes, and shrimp and with Spain's distinctive pimentón de La Vera, a smoked paprika. A sprinkle of crispy bacon pieces and crumbled blue cheese adds additional flavor.

To make the vinaigrette, combine the mayonnaise, sour cream, olive oil, vinegar, mustard, and garlic in a food processor or blender and process until smooth. Set aside. (The vinaigrette can be made up to 1 day in advance, covered tightly, and refrigerated. Bring to room temperature before using.)

In a large bowl, toss together the shrimp, olive oil, paprika, and a little salt and pepper. Preheat a large, nonstick frying pan over medium-high heat. Add half of the shrimp and sauté until they turn pink and are opaque throughout, about 3 minutes. Transfer to a large bowl and repeat with the remaining shrimp. Set aside to cool.

Rinse the frying pan, wipe dry, and return to medium heat. Add the bacon slices and fry, turning as needed, until crisp, about 6 minutes. Using a slotted spatula, transfer to paper towels to drain. Let cool, then crumble and set aside.

To assemble the slaw, add the cabbage, celery, green onions, radishes, parsley, and vinaigrette to the shrimp and toss to coat all the ingredients evenly. Season to taste with salt and pepper and toss again.

Transfer the slaw to a serving bowl or deep platter. Sprinkle the crumbled bacon and the blue cheese, if using, over the top. Serve at once.

Serves 8

CREAMY CIDER VINAIGRETTE

1/2 cup (4 fl oz/125 ml) mayonnaise

1/4 cup (2 oz/60 g) sour cream or
1/4 cup (2 fl oz/60 ml) buttermilk

1/4 cup (2 fl oz/60 ml) olive oil

1/4 cup (2 fl oz/60 ml) unfiltered
cider vinegar

1 teaspoon dry mustard

1 clove garlic, chopped

2 lb (1 kg) shrimp (prawns), peeled
and deveined

3 tablespoons olive oil

1 teaspoon mild Spanish smoked
paprika, *pimentón de La Vera*

Coarse salt and freshly ground pepper

1/4 lb (125 g) apple wood–smoked
bacon slices

1/2 head green cabbage, cored
and shredded

5 celery stalks, thinly sliced

6 green (spring) onions, including
tender green tops, chopped

1 bunch red radishes, trimmed and
thinly sliced

1/2 cup (3/4 oz/20 g) chopped fresh
flat-leaf (Italian) parsley

1/3 cup (2 oz/60 g) crumbled blue
cheese, preferably Maytag (optional)

FIRE-ROASTED CORN SALAD

Juice of 3 limes

2 teaspoons ground cumin

1 teaspoon mild chili powder

3/4 cup (6 fl oz/180 ml) extra-virgin olive oil, plus more for brushing

Coarse salt and freshly ground pepper

6 ears corn, shucked

3 cups (18 oz/560 g) cherry tomatoes, stems removed and halved

1/2 cup (2 oz/60 g) diced red onion

1/2 cup (3/4 oz/20 g) chopped fresh cilantro (fresh coriander)

1/4 lb (125 g) feta cheese, diced

2 teaspoons cumin seeds, toasted and lightly crushed

Fresh corn is best between the months of July and September, making it a popular vegetable for a summer barbecue. Try it grilled and folded into this salad with bright cherry tomatoes and tangy feta cheese.

In a bowl, whisk together the lime juice, ground cumin, and chili powder. Stream in the 3/4 cup oil while whisking to make a vinaigrette. Season with salt and pepper.

Prepare a charcoal or gas grill for direct grilling over medium-high heat. Brush a little olive oil on each ear of corn. Grill the corn, turning the ears often so that they cook evenly, until lightly charred, about 10 minutes.

Steady each corn ear on a cutting board and, using a sharp knife, cut down along the cob to strip off the kernels. Put the kernels in a large bowl. Add the tomatoes, onion, cilantro, feta, and the vinaigrette and toss to coat evenly. Transfer the salad to a platter and sprinkle with the cumin seeds. Serve at once.

GRILLED POTATO SALAD

2 cups (2 oz/60 g) fresh flat-leaf (Italian) parsley leaves

1/4 cup (2 oz/60 g) capers

2 cloves garlic, chopped

1 tablespoon Dijon mustard

2 tablespoons red wine vinegar

1/4 cup (2 fl oz/60 ml) extra-virgin olive oil, plus 2 tablespoons

Coarse salt and freshly ground pepper

2 lb (1 kg) fingerling potatoes, each about 1 inch (2.5 cm) in diameter, boiled until almost tender

Fingerling potatoes, named for their long, slender profile, are relatively small and irregularly shaped and have a dense, creamy yellow interior. Their size and texture make them a good choice for grilling.

In a food processor, combine the parsley, capers, garlic, mustard, and vinegar and pulse until coarsely chopped. Slowly stream in the 1/4 cup olive oil, pulsing just until the parsley mixture is well blended but still has a coarse texture. Season with 1 teaspoon salt and pepper to taste. Transfer to a large bowl.

Prepare a charcoal or gas grill for direct grilling over medium-high heat. Rub the potatoes with the 2 tablespoons olive oil and thread them onto metal skewers. Grill the potatoes, turning occasionally, until tender, 5–10 minutes.

Slide the potatoes off the skewers onto a cutting board and cut into slices 1/4 inch (6 mm) thick. Transfer the potato slices to the bowl holding the parsley mixture and toss well. Season to taste with salt and pepper, toss again, and serve.

Each recipe serves 8

LEMON-HERB CHICKEN BREASTS

It is generally a good idea to offer a choice of at least two different grilled meats when hosting a barbecue, and you usually cannot go wrong making chicken one of them. Chicken breasts marinated in lemon and herbs are a nice contrast to the baby back ribs also featured on the menu.

Rinse the chicken breasts and pat dry. In a large, shallow nonreactive dish, whisk together the olive oil, garlic, grated lemon zest and juice, the 2 tablespoons rosemary, thyme, 2 teaspoons salt, and 1 teaspoon pepper. Add the chicken breasts and turn to coat well. Cover and refrigerate for at least 4 hours or for up to 8 hours.

Prepare a charcoal or gas grill for direct grilling over medium-high heat. Oil the grill rack and position it about 6 inches (15 cm) from the heat source.

Grill the chicken breasts, turning once, until firm to the touch and opaque throughout, about 5 minutes on each side. Transfer the chicken breasts to a cutting board and cut on the diagonal against the grain into slices $1/2$ inch (12 mm) thick. Capture any carving juices, if possible.

Arrange the chicken slices on a warmed serving platter and drizzle any carving juices over the top. To garnish, sprinkle with rosemary leaves and sprigs and shredded lemon zest, if desired.

Serves 8

3 lb (1.5 kg) boneless, skinless chicken breast halves

$1/4$ cup (2 fl oz/60 ml) extra-virgin olive oil

3 cloves garlic, finely chopped

Grated zest and juice of 1 lemon, plus shredded zest for garnish (optional)

2 tablespoons chopped fresh rosemary, plus whole leaves and sprigs for garnish (optional)

2 tablespoons chopped fresh thyme

Coarse salt and freshly ground pepper

CHIPOTLE SPICE PASTE

4 chipotle chiles packed in adobo sauce, seeded and chopped

4 cloves garlic, finely chopped

2 tablespoons tomato paste

2 tablespoons balsamic vinegar

2 tablespoons firmly packed brown sugar

1½ tablespoons sweet Spanish paprika

1½ tablespoons ground cumin

1½ tablespoons dried oregano

1½ tablespoons dried thyme

1 teaspoon ground cloves

Coarse salt

3 slabs baby back pork ribs, about 6 lb (3 kg) total weight

1 cup (8 fl oz/250 ml) store-bought mild barbecue sauce

CHIPOTLE BABY BACK RIBS

Chipotles, which are dried and smoked jalapeño chiles, add a wonderful smoky-sweet flavor to food. They are commonly packed in adobo sauce, a vinegary tomato mixture that accents the chiles' flavor. The rich, sweet meat of pork baby back ribs is a nice foil to the chiles' smoke and heat.

To prepare the spice paste, combine the chiles, garlic, tomato paste, vinegar, brown sugar, paprika, cumin, oregano, thyme, cloves, and 2 teaspoons salt in a food processor. Pulse until a smooth paste forms.

Brush the paste over the ribs, coating them evenly on both sides. The ribs can be cooked now, or, for a more intense flavor, cover them loosely with plastic wrap and refrigerate them overnight.

Preheat the oven to 275°F (135°C). If the ribs have been refrigerated, remove them from the refrigerator 15 minutes before cooking. Place the ribs in a single layer on a rimmed baking sheet, overlapping them slightly if needed. Roast, turning occasionally, until tender, about 2 hours. (The ribs can be prepared up to this point a day in advance, covered, and refrigerated. Bring the ribs to room temperature before continuing.)

Prepare a charcoal or gas grill for direct grilling over medium-high heat. Oil the grill rack and position it about 6 inches (15 cm) from the heat source. Brush the ribs with ½ cup (4 fl oz/125 ml) of the barbecue sauce. Grill the ribs, turning once, until heated through, about 5 minutes on each side. Transfer the slabs to a cutting board and cut into 1-rib portions.

Arrange the ribs on a platter, brush with the remaining ½ cup barbecue sauce, and serve at once.

Serves 8

BERRY COBBLER

The variety of berries and the amount of each type you use for this simple, yet satisfying cobbler will depend on what looks good at the market. This basic recipe can also be used for other seasonal fruit cobblers: use 6 to 8 peeled and sliced apples in autumn or peaches in midsummer.

Preheat the oven to 375°F (190°C). Lightly butter a 9-by-13-inch (23-by-33-cm) baking dish.

In a bowl, combine the berries, lemon juice, ¹/₂ cup granulated sugar, cornstarch, cinnamon, and ground ginger and toss to coat the berries evenly. Pour the berry mixture into the prepared baking dish, spreading it evenly.

To make the topping in a food processor, combine the flour, brown sugar, baking powder, salt, and baking soda and pulse briefly to mix. Add the butter and pulse until the mixture resembles coarse meal. In a small bowl, whisk together the egg and cream. Pour the egg mixture into the food processor and pulse just until the topping mixture holds together. Remove the blade from the food processor and stir in the crystallized ginger.

To make the topping by hand, in a bowl, stir together the flour, brown sugar, baking powder, salt, and baking soda. Scatter the butter pieces over the top and, using a pastry blender or 2 knives, cut in the butter until the mixture resembles coarse meal. In a small bowl, whisk together the egg and cream. Slowly pour the egg mixture into the flour mixture, stirring and tossing with a fork until the topping mixture holds together. Stir in the crystallized ginger.

Using a soup spoon, place dollops of the topping evenly over the berries, leaving a 1-inch (2.5-cm) border uncovered around the edge of the dish. Sprinkle the 3 tablespoons granulated sugar over the top. Place the dish on a rimmed baking sheet. Bake the cobbler until the top is golden and the berry filling is bubbling, about 35 minutes. Transfer to a wire rack and let cool for 10–15 minutes.

With a large spoon or spatula, scoop out the cobbler onto individual plates and serve. Accompany with a scoop of vanilla ice cream, if desired.

Serves 8

2 lb (1 kg) mixed berries

Juice of 1 lemon

¹/₂ cup (4 oz/125 g) granulated sugar, plus 3 tablespoons

2 tablespoons cornstarch (cornflour)

¹/₂ teaspoon ground cinnamon

1 teaspoon ground ginger

COBBLER TOPPING

2¹/₄ cups (11¹/₂ oz/360 g) unbleached all-purpose (plain) flour

¹/₂ cup (3¹/₂ oz/105 g) firmly packed golden brown sugar

2 teaspoons baking powder

1 teaspoon salt

1 teaspoon baking soda (bicarbonate of soda)

6 tablespoons (3 oz/90 g) chilled unsalted butter, cut into ¹/₂-inch (12-mm) pieces

1 large egg

³/₄ cup (6 fl oz/180 ml) heavy (double) cream

¹/₄ cup (1¹/₂ oz/45 g) finely minced crystallized ginger

Vanilla ice cream for serving (optional)

SEASIDE SUPPER

When the setting for a meal is as dramatic as it is beautiful, little decoration is needed. For a summertime seafood feast on the deck of a beach house, the table is set in shades of lavender and periwinkle that reflect the calm of the evening sea and sky and provide a gentle contrast to the color of the dunes. The linens are anchored with

heavy hurricane lamps and with seashells, which are also used as salt and pepper cellars. You can also re-create this menu and table setting on a backyard patio, adding a few vases filled with sprays of beach grass to recall the carefree mood of an evening by the shore.

TIPS FOR BEACHSIDE DINING

- For an easy, refreshing hors d'oeuvre, wrap thin slices of *serrano* ham around fresh figs or melon.

- Arrange comfortable chairs and small tables facing the water for guests to mingle and enjoy the view.

- To anchor the tablecloth against the wind, tie small shells or beach pebbles to each corner.

- Place small shellfish forks above the plate or to the left of the dinner fork to assist in eating the mollusks.

MENU

Summer Vegetable Gazpacho

Garlic Toasts

Spanish-Style Steamed Shellfish

Flan with Fresh Figs

White Rioja

WORK PLAN

AT LEAST ONE DAY IN ADVANCE

Make the gazpacho and balsamic syrup

Purée the *romesco* sauce for the shellfish dish

THE DAY OF THE PARTY

Prepare the vegetables and scrub
the mollusks for the shellfish dish

Bake the flan

JUST BEFORE SERVING

Make the toasts

Finish the shellfish dish

HERB-INFUSED HAND TOWELS

Hand towels, perfumed with lemon and herbs, are always welcome after eating food with your hands. Rolled and tied in advance, these cloths are steeped in a warm lemon-herb infusion just before you offer them to your guests.

roll cotton napkins, facecloths, or tea towels into cylinders. If desired, tie them with beach grass for a decorative touch.

pour the herbal infusion into a wide, heatproof bowl filled with lemon slices and let stand for about 10 seconds.

steep fresh herbs, such as rosemary or mint, in boiling water in a teapot for 2 to 3 minutes.

soak the rolled napkins in the infusion. When cool enough to handle, wring them out slightly and arrange on a tray.

Summer Vegetable Gazpacho

In Spain, the vegetables for this chilled soup are traditionally warmed in the summer sun, to release their flavors. It is also common to season the soup with a little of the famed local smoked paprika.

Peel, seed, and finely chop the tomatoes and cucumber. Finely chop the onion. Seed and finely chop the bell peppers. In a large, nonreactive bowl, combine the bread slices and 1/2 cup (4 fl oz/125 ml) of the tomato juice and let stand for 10 minutes. Stir in the tomatoes, cucumber, onion, yellow and red bell peppers, garlic, broth, the remaining 2¹/₂ cups (20 fl oz/625 ml) tomato juice, 2 tablespoons each olive oil and balsamic syrup, paprika, and cumin, mixing well. Season to taste with salt and pepper. Cover loosely with plastic wrap and let stand at room temperature for 1 hour to blend the flavors.

Transfer 4 cups (32 fl oz/1 l) of the tomato mixture to a blender and process until smooth. Return the puréed mixture to the bowl, stirring well. Cover and refrigerate until chilled, at least 4 hours or for up to 24 hours. When ready to serve, in a small bowl, stir together the cilantro, mint, and lemon zest. Ladle the soup into chilled bowls and sprinkle each serving with an equal amount of the shredded herb mixture. Drizzle a little olive oil and balsamic syrup over each serving.

2 lb (1 kg) ripe tomatoes

1 English (hothouse) cucumber

1 red onion

1 *each* yellow and red bell pepper (capsicum)

3 slices day-old sourdough French bread, crusts removed and torn

3 cups (24 fl oz/750 ml) tomato juice

2 cloves garlic, minced

3 cups (24 fl oz/750 ml) vegetable broth

2 tablespoons extra-virgin olive oil, plus more for garnish

2 tablespoons balsamic syrup (page 103), plus more for garnish

1 tablespoon mild smoked Spanish paprika, *pimentón de La Vera*

1 teaspoon ground cumin

Coarse salt and freshly ground pepper

2 tablespoons *each* finely shredded fresh cilantro (fresh coriander) and mint

1 tablespoon finely chopped lemon zest

Garlic Toasts

These toasts, fragrant with garlic and olive oil, do double duty: they accompany both the first-course soup and the main-course shellfish dish. Keep them warm, wrapped in aluminum foil, in a 200°F (95°C) oven.

Preheat the broiler (grill). In a small bowl, stir together the olive oil and garlic. Lightly brush both sides of each bread slice with some of the oil and arrange the slices in a single layer on rimmed baking sheets.

Place the baking sheets under the broiler 5 inches (13 cm) from the heat source and toast until golden brown on the first side, about 30 seconds. Turn the slices and toast the second side until golden brown, about 30 seconds longer.

Each recipe serves 6

1/4 cup (2 fl oz/60 ml) olive oil

1 clove garlic, crushed

2 loaves crusty French bread, 1 lb (500 g) each, cut into slices 1/2 inch (12 mm) thick

SPANISH-STYLE STEAMED SHELLFISH

ROMESCO SAUCE

1/2 cup (3 oz/90 g) whole almonds

3 cloves garlic

1 slice French bread, torn into pieces

2 ripe plum (Roma) tomatoes, halved

1/3 cup (2 oz/60 g) chopped roasted red bell pepper (capsicum)

1/2 teaspoon mild smoked paprika

2 tablespoons sherry vinegar

1/2 cup (4 fl oz/125 ml) fruity extra-virgin olive oil

Coarse salt

Coarse salt and freshly ground pepper

1/2 lb (250 g) tender green beans

9 small new potatoes, halved

2 carrots, peeled and cut into chunks

2 tablespoons extra-virgin olive oil

1/2 lb (250 g) Spanish chorizo, sliced

1 teaspoon saffron threads

1 leek, with tender green tops, chopped

1 fennel bulb, trimmed, cored, and thinly sliced lengthwise

2 cloves garlic, chopped

1 orange zest strip, 3 inches (7.5 cm) long by 1 inch (2.5 cm) wide

2 cups (16 fl oz/500 ml) reduced-sodium chicken broth

1 cup (8 fl oz/250 ml) dry white wine

3 frozen lobster tails, 1/2 lb (250 g) each, thawed and halved lengthwise

12 large shrimp (prawns) in the shell

18 mussels, green-lipped if available, scrubbed and debearded

24 Manila clams, scrubbed

Chopped fresh flat-leaf (Italian) parsley for garnish

Ingredients traditionally used in Spanish seafood stews are brought together here. Spanish chorizo and saffron flavor the broth, and a classic red pepper–based romesco *sauce provides a tangy accent.*

To make the *romesco*, preheat the oven to 450°F (230°C). Arrange the nuts, garlic, bread, tomatoes, pepper, and paprika in a single layer on a rimmed baking sheet. Roast until the edges of the tomatoes and the bread start to brown, about 10 minutes. Transfer to a food processor and pulse to coarsely chop. Slowly add the vinegar and oil and process until mixed, but not completely smooth. Season with salt. (The sauce can be prepared up to 1 day in advance, covered, and refrigerated.)

Bring a saucepan three-fourths full of salted water to a boil over high heat. Add the green beans and cook until tender, about 5 minutes. Drain, refresh with running cold water, and set aside. In another saucepan, cook the potatoes and carrots in the same way until tender, about 12 minutes. Drain and set aside.

In a large Dutch oven over medium heat, warm the 2 tablespoons olive oil. Add the chorizo and sauté until golden, about 5 minutes. Drain the chorizo on paper towels and pour off all but 3 tablespoons of the fat from the pot. Return the pot to medium heat, add the saffron, leek, fennel, and garlic, and sauté for 3 minutes. Stir in the orange zest, broth, and wine and bring to a simmer. Reduce the heat to medium-low and cook until reduced by one-third, about 15 minutes.

Place the lobster tail halves in the pot, cover, and cook until the shells are bright red and the meat is almost cooked through, about 8 minutes. Uncover and layer the following ingredients in order: shrimp, mussels, clams, potatoes, carrots, green beans, and chorizo, discarding any mussels or clams that do not close to the touch. Season with salt and pepper, cover, and cook until the mussels and clams have opened and the vegetables are heated through, 5–7 minutes.

To serve, remove the lobster meat from the shells and place a half tail in the center of each warmed shallow bowl. Arrange the potatoes, carrots, green beans, chorizo, mussels, shrimp, and clams in equal portions around the lobster meat, discarding any shellfish that failed to open. Ladle some of the cooking liquid over each serving and top with a spoonful of the *romesco* sauce and a little parsley. Serve at once.

Serves 6

FLAN WITH FRESH FIGS

Caramelized figs crown this rich and creamy, vanilla-scented flan. Buy the figs just before you need them, as they spoil quickly, and select fruits that give slightly to the touch, ensuring that they are ripe but not too soft.

In a saucepan over medium heat, combine the cream, granulated sugar, and vanilla bean and bring to a gentle simmer, stirring to dissolve the sugar. Remove from the heat and set aside for 30 minutes.

In a frying pan over medium-high heat, melt the butter. Stir in the brown sugar until dissolved, about 1 minute. Add the fig pieces and cook until soft, about 12 minutes. Remove from the heat. Arrange the figs in the bottom of a round, nonstick 9-inch (23-cm) cake pan, spreading the pieces in a single layer and covering the bottom evenly with the syrup. Place the pan in the freezer for 15 minutes.

Preheat the oven to 375°F (190°C). Retrieve the vanilla bean halves from the cream and, using the tip of a small knife, scrape the seeds into the cream. Discard the bean halves. Place the pan over medium heat and bring to a simmer; keep warm.

In a large bowl, combine the whole eggs, egg yolks, and salt. Using an electric mixer on medium speed, beat until smooth. Slowly pour in the warm cream mixture while continuing to beat on medium speed until well combined. Pour the egg mixture through a fine-mesh sieve into the cake pan, being careful not to dislodge the figs. Place the pan in a roasting pan. Pour in boiling water to reach halfway up the side of the cake pan. Place a sheet of aluminum foil loosely over the cake pan.

Bake the flan until a knife inserted into the center comes out clean, about 40 minutes. Remove the cake pan from the roasting pan, place on a wire rack, and let cool to room temperature, at least 2 hours. Cover and refrigerate until ready to serve. (You can make the recipe up to this point 1 day in advance.)

To serve, run a thin-bladed knife blade around the edge of the flan to loosen it from the pan sides. Immerse the bottom of the cake pan in a pan of hot water for about 3 seconds to loosen the caramel. Invert a large serving plate over the top, and invert the pan and plate in a single quick motion. Tap the bottom of the pan lightly with the handle of the knife to loosen the flan, then lift off the pan. Serve at once.

Serves 6

3 cups (24 fl oz/750 ml) heavy (double) cream

3/4 cup (6 oz/185 g) granulated sugar

1 vanilla bean, split lengthwise

2 tablespoons unsalted butter

1/4 cup (2 oz/60 g) firmly packed golden brown sugar

6 Black Mission figs, stems removed and cut in half lengthwise

4 large whole eggs, plus 4 large egg yolks

1/4 teaspoon salt

AUTUMN

MENUS FOR AUTUMN

PIZZA PARTY

Make-Your-Own Pizza Dough

Four Pizza Ideas

Four Pizza Toppings

Cornmeal Cake with Cherry Compote

164

MIDDAY TEA PARTY

Perfect Pot of Tea

Assorted Tea Sandwiches

Currant Scones

Apple-Walnut Tea Cakes

180

WINE LOVERS' EVENING

Dates Stuffed with Goat Cheese

Riesling Onion Soup with Herbed Croutons

Seared Duck Breast with Pinot Noir Sauce

Potato and Apple Galette

Savoy Cabbage and Turnips

Pear, Endive, and Walnut Salad

Selection of Artisanal Cheeses

Individual Orange Butter Cakes

196

THANKSGIVING FEAST

Carrot Soup with Bacon and Chestnut Cream

Sage-Rubbed Turkey

Bread and Sausage Stuffing

Pear and Cranberry Chutney

Sweet Potato Purée

Green Beans with Almonds

Barley Pilaf with Chanterelles

Pumpkin Pie with Candied Pecans

218

PIZZA PARTY

Some dinner parties are especially easy, others are particularly fun. This casual, make-your-own-pizza dinner, set right in the kitchen, is both. The host makes the dough and the toppings ahead of time, and the guests join in the cooking, assembling their own pizzas for everyone to try. There's no formal seating area. Instead, friends

gather around the kitchen island to eat standing up or sitting on stools. Kids enjoy this party, too, because they get to create pizzas suited to their taste. All the ingredients are put out in advance on colorful platters, creating a cheery Mediterranean-inspired feeling of abundance.

TIPS FOR PIZZA PARTIES

- Divide the tasks among the guests: have one shape the dough rounds and the others top and bake the pizzas.

- Round out a pizza menu with a simple tossed green salad, olives, cheeses, bread sticks, and fruit.

- Instead of a set table, stand flatware in tumblers on the kitchen island.

- Pile extra vegetables in a simple bowl to act as a casual centerpiece.

- Have heavy-duty aluminum foil on hand to pack up any leftover pizza for guests to take home.

MENU

Make-Your-Own Pizza Dough

Four Pizza Ideas

Four Pizza Toppings

Cornmeal Cake with Cherry Compote

Zinfandel

WORK PLAN

AT LEAST ONE DAY IN ADVANCE

Make the cherry compote

Make the pizza dough

THE DAY OF THE PARTY

Prepare the pizza toppings

Bake the cake

JUST BEFORE SERVING

Put out the balls of pizza dough
and the toppings

TOPIARY PARTY FAVORS

This simple idea turns a miniature topiary (or any potted plant) into a special gift that you can use to thank the guests for their cooking help. The idea also works well as a host gift, in place of the predictable flowers or bottle of wine.

organize all the necessary supplies: a small plant, preferably one with a single tall stem (here, a rosemary topiary); a decorative pot; sheer fabric; complementary ribbon; pinking shears; and a gift tag.

place the plant in its new pot, and set it on the fabric. Cut the fabric with the pinking shears (for a decorative edge and to keep the fabric from unraveling) into a square large enough to wrap the pot.

gather the fabric around the pot, pleating it evenly; secure with ribbon, tying it around the plant's stem. Attach a gift tag with a message on the front and care instructions on the back.

MAKE-YOUR-OWN PIZZA DOUGH

Preparing pizza dough from scratch is simple. A few ingredients, probably already on hand in your pantry, combine to make a canvas on which your guests can create their own delicious works of art. Have all the pizza toppings lined up in bowls so that the choices are easily visible.

To make the dough, pour the warm water into the bowl of a stand mixer. Sprinkle the yeast over the top and let stand until slightly foamy, about 5 minutes. Place the bowl on the mixer fitted with the dough hook. Add $^1/_2$ cup ($2^1/_2$ oz/75 g) of the flour and the salt; mix until combined. Add the remaining flour about $^1/_2$ cup at a time, continuing to mix until all of the flour is incorporated. Knead with the dough hook until the dough is smooth but not sticky, about 10 minutes.

Transfer the dough to a work surface and divide in half. Shape each half into a round, then place each in a large zippered plastic bag coated in olive oil. Press out any excess air. Place the dough balls in the refrigerator overnight. They should rise slowly until they have doubled in bulk.

When ready to bake the pizzas, remove the dough from the refrigerator and divide each ball into 4 equal balls. Transfer the balls to a baking sheet and allow to come to room temperature, about 1 hour.

Preheat the oven to 450°F (230°C). If using a baking stone, place it on the center oven rack to preheat. Dust a work surface with the remaining flour. Working with 1 ball at a time, and using your hand, begin to press it out gently into a round. Then, place one hand in the center of the dough and pull, lift, and stretch the dough with the other hand, gradually working around the edge until the round is $^1/_4$ inch (6 mm) thick and about 12 inches (30 cm) in diameter. Flip the dough over from time to time as you shape it. Lift the edge of the round to form a slight rim.

To bake each pizza, dust a baker's peel (or a rimless baking sheet) with cornmeal, and place a dough round on it. Top as desired. Carefully slide the topped pizza onto the baking stone. (If using a rimmed baking sheet rather than a stone, top the round directly on the baking sheet and place the sheet in the oven.) Bake until the crust is crisp and lightly golden and the topping looks ready, about 12 minutes. Remove from the oven, cut into 8 wedges, and serve immediately.

Makes eight 12-inch (30-cm) pizzas; serves 8

2$^3/_4$ cups (22 fl oz/680 ml) lukewarm water

3 tablespoons active dry yeast

8$^1/_4$ cups (2$^1/_2$ lb/1.25 kg) all-purpose (plain) flour, plus 1$^1/_2$ cups (7$^1/_2$ oz/ 235 g) for working

1 tablespoon salt

Olive oil

Cornmeal for dusting

Four Pizza Toppings (page 177)

Four Pizza Ideas

PROSCIUTTO AND ARUGULA PIZZAS

2 pizza dough rounds (page 173)

6 oz (185 g) Asiago cheese, thinly sliced

4 oz (125 g) thinly sliced prosciutto

2 cups (2 oz/60 g) arugula (rocket)
leaves, torn into bite-sized pieces

1 tablespoon extra-virgin olive oil

Freshly ground pepper

POTATO AND MUSHROOM PIZZAS

2 pizza dough rounds (page 173)

Roasted Fingerling Potatoes (page 177)

Sautéed Mushrooms (page 177)

1/2 lb (250 g) small, fresh mozzarella
cheese balls

1 tablespoon fresh rosemary leaves

1 tablespoon extra-virgin olive oil

White truffle oil (optional)

EGGPLANT AND PEPPER PIZZAS

2 pizza dough rounds (page 173)

Roasted Eggplant Slices (page 177)

1/2 cup (2 oz/60 g) roasted red bell
pepper (capsicum) strips

6 oz (185 g) Italian fontina cheese,
shredded

1 tablespoon extra-virgin olive oil

1 tablespoon fresh oregano leaves

OVEN-DRIED TOMATO PIZZAS

2 pizza dough rounds (page 173)

Oven-Dried Tomatoes (page 177)

5 oz (155 g) goat cheese, crumbled

1/4 cup (1/4 oz/7 g) torn fresh basil
leaves

1 tablespoon extra-virgin olive oil

Each of these recipes will yield two pizzas. Set out additional topping ingredients, such as a variety of cheeses, fresh herbs, olives, and cured meats, for guests who want to create their own pizza combinations.

Preheat the oven as directed in Make-Your-Own Pizzas on page 173.

To make the prosciutto and arugula pizzas, place a dough round on a baker's peel or baking sheet as directed. Scatter half each of the cheese, prosciutto, and arugula evenly over the top of the dough. Drizzle with half of the olive oil and sprinkle with a little ground pepper. Slide the pizza onto the pizza stone or place the baking sheet in the oven, and bake as directed. Repeat with the remaining dough round and topping ingredients.

To make the potato and mushroom pizzas, place a dough round on a baker's peel or baking sheet as directed. Scatter half each of the potatoes, mushrooms, and mozzarella pieces evenly over the top of the dough. Sprinkle with half of the rosemary. Drizzle with half of the olive oil. Slide the pizza onto the pizza stone or place the baking sheet in the oven, and bake as directed. If desired, drizzle the pizza with a few drops of truffle oil after it comes out of the oven. Repeat with the remaining dough round and topping ingredients.

To make the eggplant and pepper pizzas, place a dough round on a baker's peel or baking sheet as directed. Scatter half each of the eggplant, red bell pepper, and cheese evenly over the top of the dough. Drizzle with half of the olive oil and sprinkle with half of the oregano. Slide the pizza onto the pizza stone or place the baking sheet in the oven, and bake as directed. Repeat with the remaining dough round and topping ingredients.

To make the oven-dried tomato pizzas, place a dough round on a baker's peel or baking sheet as directed. Scatter half each of the tomatoes, cheese, and basil leaves evenly over the top of the dough. Drizzle with half of the olive oil. Slide the pizza onto the pizza stone or place the baking sheet in the oven, and bake as directed. Repeat with the remaining dough round and topping ingredients.

Makes eight 12-inch (30-cm) pizzas; serves 8

Four Pizza Toppings

Here are four toppings used on the pizzas on page 174. Guests can also mix these same toppings with other ingredients to make different pizzas. For example, they might combine the potatoes with thinly sliced onions and rosemary, or the eggplant and tomatoes with olives and capers.

To prepare the fingerling potatoes, preheat the oven to 425°F (220°C). Put the potatoes in a bowl, add the extra-virgin olive oil, and season lightly with salt and pepper. Toss well to coat the potatoes. Transfer to a small roasting pan. Roast the potatoes, turning occasionally, until browned and tender, 20–30 minutes. Remove from the oven, let cool slightly, and then carefully cut crosswise into thin slices. Place the slices in a shallow bowl and season to taste with salt and pepper.

To prepare the mushrooms, in a large frying pan over medium-high heat, melt the butter with the 1 tablespoon olive oil. Add the mushrooms and thyme and season to taste with salt and pepper. Cook, stirring frequently and adding more oil if the mushrooms begin to scorch, until the mushrooms are browned, about 10 minutes. Transfer to a shallow bowl and let cool.

To prepare the eggplant slices, preheat the oven to 425°F (220°C). Oil a large rimmed baking sheet with 2 tablespoons of the olive oil. Cut each eggplant half crosswise into slices ¼ inch (6 mm) thick. Lay the slices in a single layer on the prepared baking sheet. Sprinkle the slices evenly with 1 teaspoon salt and set aside for 15 minutes. Using paper towels, wipe the excess moisture from the surface of the eggplant slices. Brush the remaining 2 tablespoons olive oil evenly over the eggplant slices. Roast until tender and lightly golden, 20–25 minutes. Remove from the oven, let cool completely on the pan, and then transfer to a plate.

To prepare the tomatoes, preheat the oven to 450°F (230°C). Lightly oil a rimmed baking sheet. Arrange the tomatoes, cut side up and in a single layer, on the prepared baking sheet. Brush the tomatoes generously with the olive oil. Sprinkle the garlic, thyme, sugar, 1 teaspoon salt, and ¼ teaspoon pepper evenly over the tomatoes. Place the tomatoes in the oven, reduce the temperature to 250°F (120°C), and bake until lightly browned and wrinkled, about 3 hours. Turn off the oven and let the tomatoes remain in the closed oven for 2 hours longer. Transfer the tomato halves to a shallow bowl and pour any pan juices over the top.

Each topping will cover two 12-inch (30-cm) pizzas

ROASTED FINGERLING POTATOES

1 lb (500 g) fingerling potatoes

2 tablespoons extra-virgin olive oil

Coarse salt and freshly ground pepper

SAUTÉED MUSHROOMS

2 tablespoons unsalted butter

1 tablespoon olive oil, or as needed

½ lb (250 g) mixed small fresh mushrooms, sliced through the stem

1 teaspoon chopped fresh thyme

Coarse salt and freshly ground pepper

ROASTED EGGPLANT SLICES

4 tablespoons (2 fl oz/60 ml) olive oil

1 eggplant (aubergine), about 1 lb (500 g), cut in half lengthwise

Coarse salt

OVEN-DRIED TOMATOES

12 plum (Roma) tomatoes, preferably 6 each red and yellow, halved lengthwise

⅓ cup (3 fl oz/80 ml) olive oil

2 cloves garlic, chopped

1 tablespoon fresh thyme leaves

2 teaspoons sugar

Coarse salt and freshly ground pepper

CORNMEAL CAKE WITH CHERRY COMPOTE

Cornmeal lends a nutty flavor and rustic texture to this easy cake. For a festive presentation, a fragrant cherry compote flavored with vin santo *is spooned over each serving. Both the cake and the compote can be made well in advance.*

COMPOTE

1 lb (500 g) dark cherries, preferably sour cherries, stems removed, pitted, and halved

1 tablespoon unsalted butter

1 tablespoon granulated sugar

1/4 cup (2 fl oz/60 ml) *vin santo*

1 teaspoon almond extract (essence)

CORNMEAL CAKE

3/4 cup (3 oz/90 g) cake (soft-wheat) flour

3/4 cup (3 oz/90 g) ground almonds

2/3 cup (3 1/2 oz/105 g) yellow cornmeal

1/2 teaspoon baking powder

1/4 teaspoon salt

1 cup (8 oz/250 g) unsalted butter, at room temperature

1 vanilla bean, split lengthwise

1 cup (8 oz/250 g) granulated sugar

3 large eggs, at room temperature

Grated zest and juice of 1 large lemon

Shredded lemon zest and confectioners' (icing) sugar for finishing

To make the compote, in a nonreactive saucepan over high heat, combine the cherries, butter, and granulated sugar and bring to a boil. Reduce the heat to low and simmer, stirring occasionally, until the cherries have begun to soften, 3–5 minutes. Remove from the heat and stir in the *vin santo* and almond extract. Return the compote to medium-low heat and cook, uncovered, until the alcohol evaporates, about 2 minutes. Remove from the heat and set aside. (The compote can be made up to 1 day in advance, cooled, covered tightly, and stored in the refrigerator. Let stand at room temperature for 1 hour before serving.)

To make the cake, preheat the oven to 350°F (180°C). Butter a 9-inch (23-cm) springform pan. Dust with flour and tap out the excess.

In a bowl, stir together the flour, almonds, cornmeal, baking powder, and salt. Set aside. Place the butter in a large bowl. Using the tip of a small knife, scrape the seeds from the vanilla bean halves into the bowl holding the butter. Using an electric mixer on medium-high speed, beat the butter until light and creamy. Gradually add the granulated sugar, beating until fluffy and ivory colored, about 2 minutes. Add the eggs one at a time, beating well after each addition. Stir in the grated lemon zest and juice. Reduce the speed to low and gradually beat in the flour mixture just until combined. Pour into the prepared pan and smooth the top.

Bake the cake until a toothpick inserted into the center comes out clean, about 1 hour. Transfer the cake to a wire rack and let cool in the pan for 10 minutes. Release and remove the pan sides. Let the cake cool completely. (The cake can be made up to 8 hours in advance, covered, and stored at room temperature.) Transfer the cake to a serving plate. Garnish the top with shredded lemon zest, then, using a fine-mesh sieve, lightly dust the top with confectioners' sugar. Cut into wedges, divide among individual plates, and spoon the compote over the top. Serve at once.

Serves 8

MIDDAY TEA PARTY

A traditional tea party has timeless appeal, and its quiet charm makes it an ideal choice for a daytime celebration, whether it is a bridal or baby shower, a book club meeting, or simply a gathering of friends. Bunches of garden roses placed around the sunlit room help to create an inviting ambience. Silver trays and flatware, Asian-inspired linens, and a pretty tea service add a feeling of gracious elegance.

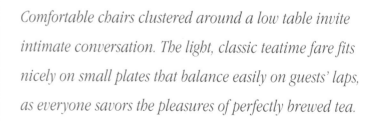

Comfortable chairs clustered around a low table invite intimate conversation. The light, classic teatime fare fits nicely on small plates that balance easily on guests' laps, as everyone savors the pleasures of perfectly brewed tea.

MENU

Perfect Pot of Tea

Assorted Tea Sandwiches

Currant Scones

Apple-Walnut Tea Cakes

WORK PLAN

AT LEAST ONE DAY IN ADVANCE

Gather a variety of loose teas

Purchase the accompaniments
for the scones

THE DAY OF THE PARTY

Bake the tea cakes

Prepare the tea sandwich ingredients:
boil the eggs; cook the shrimp, if necessary;
chop the herbs; and toast the walnuts

JUST BEFORE SERVING

Bake the scones

Assemble the tea sandwiches

TIPS FOR TEA PARTIES

- Serve tea in a comfortable seating area.

- Arrange sugar cubes, lemon slices, and a small pitcher of milk on a tray; provide a small set of tongs for the sugar cubes.

- Use a tea cozy to keep the pot warm, or drape it with a neatly folded dish towel.

- Arrange tea sandwiches decoratively on a tiered plate stand.

Take-Home Tea Sachets

Send friends home with a memento of their afternoon together: samples of the teas served at the party, packed in quantities for making single pots. For a special touch, add a second label on the back with brewing instructions for the perfect pot of tea.

select a few varieties of loose-leaf teas and arrange them on a work surface with small glassine envelopes, ribbon, decorative labels, a hole punch, and a pen.

fold the top ½ inch (12 mm) of the glassine envelope over itself and seal the packet with a label that denotes the type of tea inside.

scoop a few tablespoons of tea into each envelope, keeping track of which type of tea goes into which envelope. Stand the pouches up to move the tea to the bottom.

punch 2 small holes at the top of the envelope. Thread a length of ribbon through the holes and tie it in a bow. Arrange the sachets on a silver tray.

warm the teapot by pouring a small amount of boiling water into it, swirling the water, letting it sit for a minute or two, and then pouring it out.

cover the pot with its lid and let the tea steep until it is the desired strength. If you have a tea cozy, place it over the pot to keep the heat from dissipating.

measure loose-leaf tea into the pot, allowing 1 teaspoon for each person, plus 1 extra teaspoon for the pot. Pour in 1 cup (8 fl oz/250 ml) boiling water per person.

strain the tea through a tea strainer into teacups with saucers. Place the strainer in its holder or on a napkin-lined plate when finished pouring.

PERFECT POT OF TEA

Tradition holds that milk is served with tea, as the heaviness of cream can mask the flavor of a high-quality brew. For best results, brew only the amount of tea needed to pour a single cup for each guest.

Spring water

2 tablespoons plus 1 teaspoon loose black tea such as orange pekoe, Earl Grey, Lapsang souchong, or an herbal tea

Milk, sugar cubes, and lemon slices for serving

Fill a teakettle with spring water and bring the water to a rolling boil. Pour a small amount of the boiling water into a teapot, swirl it around, put the lid in place, and then let the water sit in the pot for about 1 minute to warm it. Pour out the water.

Add the loose tea to the pot and fill the pot with about 6 cups (48 fl oz/1.5 l) boiling water. Put the lid in place. If you have a tea cozy, place it over the pot to keep the tea hot as it brews. Let the tea steep for 2–7 minutes, depending on the type of tea you are brewing and how strong you prefer it. Green teas are steeped relatively briefly, while black teas and oolong teas are generally steeped longer.

Pour the tea through a tea strainer into each cup. Set out the milk, sugar, and lemon slices for guests to add to their cups as desired.

Serves 6

Assorted Tea Sandwiches

Tea sandwiches, like those you might find in a British-style teahouse, should be as petite and thin as possible. Loaves of thinly sliced sandwich bread, available at most grocery stores, are perfect for making these traditional teatime offerings.

To make the cucumber-watercress sandwiches, using paper towels, pat the cut surfaces of the cucumber slices to remove any excess moisture. Lightly butter one side of each bread slice. Scatter the watercress leaves evenly over all of the buttered bread slices. Layer the cucumber slices over the watercress leaves on 4 of the bread slices. Top the cucumber with some of the sprouts, if using, and a pinch of salt. Top with the remaining 4 bread slices, buttered side down.

To make the curried shrimp and egg salad sandwiches, peel and finely chop the eggs. In a bowl, combine the shrimp, eggs, celery, dill, curry powder, and mayonnaise and mix well. Season to taste with salt and pepper. Lightly butter one side of each bread slice. Divide the shrimp and egg salad evenly among 4 of the bread slices, spreading it in an even layer. Top with the remaining 4 bread slices, buttered side down.

To make the roast beef, blue cheese, and walnut sandwiches, in a small bowl, combine the butter and blue cheese and blend with a fork until smooth. Lightly spread one side of each bread slice with the butter–blue cheese mixture. Layer the sliced roast beef over 4 of the buttered bread slices and sprinkle the walnuts evenly over the beef. Top with the remaining 4 bread slices, buttered side down.

Using a sharp knife, cut off the crusts from each sandwich and then slice the sandwiches in half, either straight down the middle or on the diagonal. If smaller portions are desired, cut each half in half again.

Arrange the sandwiches on separate plates on a tiered plate stand, or on a platter. Serve at once.

Serves 6

CUCUMBER-WATERCRESS SANDWICHES

32 thin slices peeled English (hothouse) cucumber

4 tablespoons (2 oz/60 g) unsalted butter, at room temperature

8 thin slices white sandwich bread

1/2 cup (1/2 oz/15 g) watercress leaves

1/2 cup (1/2 oz/15 g) radish, onion, or sunflower sprouts (optional)

Coarse salt, preferably *fleur de sel*

CURRIED SHRIMP AND EGG SALAD SANDWICHES

2 hard-boiled eggs

6 oz (185 g) cooked, peeled shrimp (prawns), finely chopped

1 celery stalk, finely chopped

1 tablespoon finely chopped fresh dill

2 teaspoons curry powder

2 tablespoons mayonnaise

Coarse salt, preferably *fleur de sel*, and freshly ground pepper

4 tablespoons (2 oz/60 g) unsalted butter, at room temperature

8 thin slices whole-wheat (wholemeal) sandwich bread

ROAST BEEF, BLUE CHEESE, AND WALNUT SANDWICHES

4 tablespoons (2 oz/60 g) unsalted butter, at room temperature

1/3 cup (2 oz/60 g) crumbled blue cheese, preferably Maytag or Stilton, at room temperature

8 thin slices white sandwich bread

1/2 lb (250 g) thinly sliced roast beef

1/4 cup (1 oz/30 g) walnut pieces, toasted and chopped

SCONES

2¹/₄ cups (11¹/₂ oz/360 g) unbleached all-purpose (plain) flour

¹/₂ cup (3¹/₂ oz/105 g) firmly packed golden brown sugar

2 teaspoons baking powder

1 teaspoon baking soda (bicarbonate of soda)

1 teaspoon salt

6 tablespoons (3 oz/90 g) chilled unsalted butter, cut into ¹/₂-inch (12-mm) pieces

1 large egg

³/₄ cup (6 fl oz/180 ml) heavy (double) cream, plus more for glazing

¹/₂ cup (3 oz/90 g) dried currants

¹/₄ cup (1¹/₂ oz/45 g) minced crystallized ginger

3 tablespoons granulated sugar

BROWN SUGAR BUTTER

¹/₂ cup (4 oz/125 g) unsalted butter, at room temperature

2 tablespoons firmly packed dark brown sugar

Currant Scones

In addition to the brown sugar butter, traditional accompaniments for scones include lemon curd, fruit preserves, marmalade, and clotted cream. Spoon them into ramekins or other decorative containers and set them on a silver tray for guests to serve themselves.

Preheat the oven to 400°F (200°C). Lightly butter a rimmed baking sheet.

To make the scones in a food processor, combine the flour, golden brown sugar, baking powder, baking soda, and salt and pulse briefly to mix. Add the butter and pulse until the mixture resembles coarse meal. In a small bowl, whisk together the egg and the ³/₄ cup cream until blended. Pour the egg mixture into the processor and pulse just until the mixture holds together.

To make the scones by hand, in a bowl, stir together the flour, golden brown sugar, baking powder, baking soda, and salt. Scatter the butter pieces over the top and, using a pastry blender or 2 knives, cut in the butter until the mixture resembles coarse meal. In a small bowl, whisk together the egg and the ³/₄ cup cream until well blended. Slowly pour the egg mixture into the flour mixture, stirring and tossing with a fork until the mixture holds together.

Turn the mixture out onto a lightly floured work surface, knead in the currants and ginger, and bring the dough together into a ball. Using a floured rolling pin, roll out the dough ¹/₂ inch (12 mm) thick. Using a fluted biscuit cutter 3 inches (7.5 cm) in diameter, cut out as many rounds as possible. Gather the scraps into a ball and roll out again. Cut out additional rounds. You should have 12 rounds in all. Transfer the rounds to the prepared baking sheet, spacing them evenly. Brush the tops lightly with cream and sprinkle evenly with the granulated sugar.

Bake the scones until golden, about 15 minutes. Transfer to a wire rack and let cool for at least 15 minutes or for up to 1 hour before serving.

Meanwhile, make the brown sugar butter: In a bowl, whisk together the butter and dark brown sugar until well combined and creamy. Pack into a crock and set aside.

Transfer the warm scones to a napkin-lined basket. Set out the brown sugar butter and the other accompaniments of choice. Serve at once.

Serves 6

APPLE-WALNUT TEA CAKES

Fluted tartlet molds are used for baking these tiny cakes, which are perfect, lightly sweet companions to a cup of tea. Miniature muffin pans lined with decorative paper liners can be used as well. A light dusting of confectioners' sugar makes for an elegant, easy garnish.

Preheat the oven to 350°F (180°C). Lightly butter twenty-four 2¹/₂-inch (6-cm) fluted tartlet molds with ⁷/₈-inch (2.2-cm) sides with the 2 tablespoons butter.

In a large bowl, sift together the flour, cinnamon, baking soda, salt, baking powder, and cloves. Stir in the walnuts. In a separate bowl, stir together the sour cream, apple, and vanilla extract until well mixed. Set both bowls aside.

In a large bowl, using an electric mixer on medium-high speed, beat together the ¹/₂ cup butter and the granulated sugar until fluffy, about 5 minutes, stopping to scrape down the sides of the bowl with a rubber spatula as needed. Add the eggs one at a time, beating well after each addition. Reduce the mixer speed to low. Add the flour mixture in 3 batches alternately with the sour cream mixture, beginning and ending with the flour mixture and stopping to scrape down the sides of the bowl between additions. Divide the batter evenly among the prepared molds. Place the molds on a rimmed baking sheet.

Bake the cakes until a toothpick inserted into the center of a cake comes out clean, about 20 minutes. Transfer to a wire rack and let cool in the molds for 15 minutes.

To unmold, run a thin-bladed knife around the edge of each mold to loosen the sides of the cakes. Using the tip of the knife, invert each cake from its mold onto the rack. (The cakes can be made up to 4 hours in advance, cooled, and stored in an airtight container at room temperature.)

Using a fine-mesh sieve, dust the cakes lightly with the confectioners' sugar. Arrange decoratively on a platter. Serve at room temperature.

Makes 24 cakes; serves 6

2 tablespoons unsalted butter for the molds, plus ¹/₂ cup (4 oz/125 g)

1 cup (4 oz/125 g) cake (soft-wheat) flour

1 teaspoon ground cinnamon

³/₄ teaspoon baking soda (bicarbonate of soda)

¹/₂ teaspoon salt

¹/₄ teaspoon baking powder

¹/₄ teaspoon ground cloves

¹/₂ cup (2 oz/60 g) finely ground walnuts

¹/₂ cup (4 oz/125 g) sour cream

1 tart green apple, peeled, halved, cored, and grated

¹/₂ teaspoon vanilla extract (essence)

1 cup (8 oz/250 g) granulated sugar

2 large eggs

Confectioners' (icing) sugar for dusting

WINE LOVERS' EVENING

At a home overlooking vineyards, friends come together at harvesttime to share a bountiful sit-down dinner that celebrates both food and wine. Clusters of wine grapes, stems of red and gold bittersweet, and vines of grape leaves in glass decanters bring the vineyard indoors. The menu

courses are matched with local wines, which progress from white to red and light to more robust, taking their cues from the elaborate fall menu. As with any great wine-inspired menu, this one includes a cheese course.

WORK PLAN

AT LEAST ONE DAY IN ADVANCE

Stuff the dates

Make the soup and the croutons

THE DAY OF THE PARTY

Marinate the duck breasts

Cut the vegetables for the sauté

Slice the pears and make the vinaigrette
for the salad

Remove the cheeses from the refrigerator

Make the crème anglaise for the cakes

JUST BEFORE SERVING

Warm the stuffed dates

Reheat and finish the soup

Make the galette and vegetables

Sear the duck and make the sauce

Assemble the salad and cheese course

Bake the cakes

MENU

Dates Stuffed with Goat Cheese

Sparkling Wine

Riesling Onion Soup with Herbed Croutons

Dry Riesling

*Seared Duck Breast with
Pinot Noir Sauce*

Potato and Apple Galette

Savoy Cabbage and Turnips

Pinot Noir

Pear, Endive, and Walnut Salad

Selection of Artisanal Cheeses

Individual Orange Butter Cakes

Orange Muscat

TIPS FOR FOOD-AND-WINE DINNERS

- Go over the menu with a savvy wine seller to get recommendations for each menu course.

- To stay with the theme, use grape or fig leaves to line the platters for the hors d'oeuvres and cheese.

- Serve the salad unaccompanied by wine. Pour the main-course wine with the cheeses.

CORK MENU HOLDERS

Printed menus at each place setting give guests a preview of the food-and-wine pairings. Created on a home computer, using a classic typeface in black or a muted color, they are printed on quality paper. In keeping with the party's theme, each menu is anchored with a wine cork.

collect an assortment of wine corks. Red wine corks are an especially good choice because they add a hint of color, but white wine corks can also be used.

cut a slit along the length of each cork using a sharp utility knife. Carefully run the blade along the cut a few times to widen it slightly.

insert a menu into the slit in each cork. If desired, insert a thumbtack at an angle into the back of each cork and stand a menu up at each place setting. The menus can also lay flat on the plates or on the table.

WINE LOVERS' EVENING

Dates Stuffed with Goat Cheese
Sparkling Wine, Anderson Valley, California

❧

Riesling-Onion Soup with Herbed Croutons
Dry Riesling, Mendocino, California

❧

Seared Duck Breast with Pinot Noir Sauce
Sautéed Savoy Cabbage and Turnips, Potato-Apple Galette
Pinot Noir, Russian River, California

❧

Pear, Endive, and Walnut Salad
Selection of Artisan Cheeses

❧

Individual Orange Butter Cakes
Orange Muscat, Central Valley, California

OPENING WINE AND DECANTING WINE

The slim waiter's corkscrew lets you remove both foil and cork quickly. Once you learn how to use this tool, the process becomes nearly effortless.

Wines are sometimes decanted to aerate them and smooth out their tannins (young wines), or to remove sediment (older wines) with the aid of a candle.

trim the foil cap by aligning the blade of the corkscrew along the top of the lip of the bottle, pressing the blade firmly as you rotate the bottle with your other hand. Remove and discard the top of the foil cap.

insert the corkscrew's spiral "worm" into the cork, taking care to align the center of the worm directly over the center of the cork. Twist the corkscrew straight down into the cork.

extract the cork by placing the lever on the rim of the bottle and pulling up on the handle while pressing down on the lever with your thumb. Wipe the bottle with a towel.

pour a small amount of wine into a glass, twisting your wrist slightly as you finish pouring to prevent drips. Smell, then taste the wine to be sure there are no off odors or flavors, then pour into the remaining glasses.

set the bottle upright a day before you plan to open it to allow any sediment to settle. Young wines can skip this step and be poured directly into the decanter, as they will have little or no sediment.

hold the decanter in one hand, at an angle, about 4 inches (10 cm) above the flame to help you see any sediment. With the other hand, carefully pour the wine into the decanter in a slow, steady stream.

light a candle—preferably a tall taper or pillar—and let it burn for a few minutes to ensure a steady flame. This step is needed when pouring older wines to illuminate any sediment that may be present.

pause when sediment starts to appear noticeable in the neck of the decanter, and carefully wipe out the sediment with a towel before proceeding. Pour the wine from the decanter into glasses.

DATES STUFFED WITH GOAT CHEESE

These stuffed dates, which pair well with a welcoming glass of dry sparkling wine, are surprisingly simple to make. Medjool dates are sweet and rich and have thick, meaty flesh, which makes them particularly suitable for stuffing.

Preheat the oven to 375°F (190°C). Lightly oil a baking dish just large enough to hold the dates in a single layer.

In a small frying pan over medium heat, warm the olive oil. Add the bread crumbs and cook, stirring constantly, until the bread crumbs are evenly golden brown, about $1^{1}/_{2}$ minutes. Remove the pan from the heat, transfer the bread crumbs to a plate, and let cool.

With a small knife, make a small lengthwise incision in each date. Carefully remove the pits. Stuff 1 teaspoon of the goat cheese into the cavity left by each date's pit. Arrange the dates, with goat cheese side facing upward, in the prepared dish. Sprinkle the bread crumbs evenly over the top. (The dates can be prepared up to this point up to 24 hours in advance. Store, tightly covered, in the refrigerator.)

Bake the dates until warmed through, 10–12 minutes. Transfer to a serving platter and serve warm.

Serves 6

1 tablespoon olive oil

2 tablespoons fine dried bread crumbs

24 large dates, preferably Medjool

$^{1}/_{4}$ lb (125 g) soft fresh goat cheese

RIESLING ONION SOUP WITH HERBED CROUTONS

The Riesling wines produced on California's Mendocino coast are light but full flavored, and they have a pure, buttery aftertaste that pairs nicely with the onions, leeks, tarragon, and fontina cheese in this recipe. Avoid Rieslings labeled "late harvest" as they are too sweet for this soup.

3 tablespoons unsalted butter

4 large yellow onions, about 2 lb (1 kg) total weight, thinly sliced

2 leeks, including pale green tops, sliced

1 clove garlic, chopped

2 tablespoons fresh tarragon leaves, chopped

3 tablespoons all-purpose (plain) flour

2 cups (16 fl oz/500 ml) Riesling (see note)

6 cups (48 fl oz/1.5 l) reduced-sodium chicken broth

Coarse salt and freshly ground pepper

HERBED CROUTONS

1/2 baguette, thinly sliced

2 tablespoons olive oil

2 tablespoons unsalted butter, melted

2 tablespoons chopped mixed fresh herbs such as tarragon, rosemary, thyme, and flat-leaf (Italian) parsley, in any combination

1/2 lb (250 g) Italian fontina cheese, cut into small cubes

In a large, wide saucepan over medium heat, melt the butter. Add the onions, leeks, garlic, and tarragon and cook, stirring often, until the onions are soft and golden, about 15 minutes. Sprinkle in the flour and cook, stirring constantly, for 3 minutes longer. Pour in the wine, bring to a simmer, and cook until reduced by half, about 10 minutes. Pour in the broth, return to a simmer, reduce the heat to low, and cook, uncovered, until reduced slightly, about 45 minutes. (The soup can be made up to this point up to 24 hours in advance and stored, tightly covered, in the refrigerator. Reheat gently before proceeding.) Season to taste with salt and pepper.

To make the croutons, preheat the oven to 300°F (150°C). Arrange the baguette slices in a single layer on a rimmed baking sheet. In a small bowl, stir together the olive oil, butter, and herbs. Lightly coat each bread slice on both sides with the oil mixture. Toast the bread in the oven, turning occasionally, until crisp and golden brown, 15–20 minutes. Remove from the oven and set aside. (The croutons can be made up to 24 hours in advance and stored, tightly covered, at room temperature.)

Preheat the broiler (grill). Arrange individual ovenproof bowls on a baking sheet and ladle the soup into the bowls. Top each serving with 2 or 3 croutons and an equal amount of the cheese. Place the baking sheet under the broiler 7 inches (18 cm) from the heat source and broil (grill) until the cheese melts, about 1 minute. Remove from the broiler and serve at once.

Serves 6

SEARED DUCK BREAST WITH PINOT NOIR SAUCE

Duck and Pinot Noir are a classic combination. Look for Muscovy duck breasts for this recipe; they are generally larger and have a lower fat-to-meat ratio than the breasts of other duck varieties. Jars of demi-glace *are sold in specialty-food stores.*

Cut each whole duck breast in half to yield 4 halves in all. Working with 1 duck breast half at a time, place it between 2 sheets of plastic wrap and, using a meat pounder or heavy frying pan, pound it to an even thickness of about 3/4 inch (2 cm). Using a sharp knife, score the skin in a diamond pattern, taking care not to cut into the meat. Place the duck breast halves in a shallow nonreactive bowl. In a small bowl, whisk together the wine, mustard, and green onions. Pour the mixture evenly over the duck breasts, then turn the breasts to coat them evenly. Cover and refrigerate for 4 hours.

Preheat the oven to 200°F (95°C). Remove the duck breasts from the marinade and pat dry with paper towels. Season them lightly with salt and pepper. In a large frying pan over medium heat, melt the butter. Place the duck breasts, skin side down, in the pan and cook until the skin is crisp and golden, about 5 minutes. Turn the breasts over and continue to cook until medium-rare, about 8 minutes longer. Transfer the duck breasts to a plate, cover loosely with aluminum foil, and place in the oven to keep warm.

To make the sauce, drain off all but 3 tablespoons of the fat from the pan and return to medium heat. Add the green onions and mushrooms and sauté until lightly browned, about 3 minutes. Stir in the wine, broth, and *demi-glace,* raise the heat to medium-high, and cook, stirring often, until the mixture is reduced by one-fourth and coats the back of a spoon, about 15 minutes. Remove from the heat and whisk in the butter. Season to taste with salt and pepper.

To serve, cut each duck breast against the grain into slices 1/2 inch (12 mm) thick. Divide the slices evenly among warmed individual plates, fanning them. Spoon the sauce over and around the slices. Serve at once.

Serves 6

2 boneless whole duck breasts (see note), about 1 1/2 lb (750 g) each

1/2 cup (4 fl oz/125 ml) Pinot Noir

1 tablespoon Dijon mustard

2 green (spring) onions, including tender green tops, chopped

Coarse salt and freshly ground pepper

2 tablespoons unsalted butter

PINOT NOIR SAUCE

3 green (spring) onions, including tender green tops, chopped

1/2 lb (250 g) small fresh shiitake mushrooms, brushed clean and stems removed

1 cup (8 fl oz/250 ml) Pinot Noir

1 cup (8 fl oz/250 ml) reduced-sodium chicken broth

3 tablespoons *demi-glace*

1 tablespoon unsalted butter

Coarse salt and freshly ground pepper

POTATO AND APPLE GALETTE

4 large russet potatoes, about 2 lb (1 kg) total weight, peeled

2 Granny Smith, pippin, or Gravenstein apples, peeled, halved, cored, and grated

1 large egg, lightly beaten

1/2 cup (2 1/2 oz/75 g) all-purpose (plain) flour

Coarse salt and freshly ground pepper

2 tablespoons unsalted butter

2 tablespoons olive oil

This simple but elegant pancake, flavored with tart apples, is served sliced into wedges, which make attractive garnishes on each main-course plate. The potato will soak up some of the fruity sauce from the duck.

Preheat the oven to 200°F (95°C). Using the large holes on a handheld grater-shredder, shred the potatoes into a colander. Press out any excess liquid, then transfer to a large bowl. Stir in the apples, egg, and flour until well mixed. Season with 1 teaspoon salt and 1/2 teaspoon pepper.

In a 12-inch (30-cm) nonstick frying pan over medium-low heat, melt the butter with the olive oil. Add the potato mixture and, using a heatproof spatula, spread it evenly, then press down on it to bind it together. Cook until golden brown on the underside, about 15 minutes. Slide the galette out of the pan onto a flat plate. Invert the pan over the plate and carefully flip the plate and pan together in one quick motion, then lift off the plate. Return the pan to the heat and continue to cook until the second side is golden brown, about 15 minutes longer.

Remove from the heat and let the galette rest in the pan for a few minutes. Transfer to a heatproof plate and place in the oven to keep warm until serving, for up to 30 minutes. Cut into 12 wedges to serve.

SAVOY CABBAGE AND TURNIPS

2 tablespoons unsalted butter

1 turnip, peeled and cut into 1/4-inch (6-mm) cubes

1 carrot, peeled and cut into 1/4-inch (6-mm) cubes

1 head savoy cabbage, about 2 lb (1 kg), cut into quarters, cored, and sliced crosswise into strips 1/4 inch (6 mm) wide

3/4 cup (6 fl oz/180 ml) low-sodium chicken broth

Coarse salt and freshly ground pepper

1 tablespoon chopped fresh flat-leaf (Italian) parsley

Curly-leaved savoy cabbage, turnip, and carrot are combined in this simple sauté of seasonal vegetables. The combination makes an ideal bed for the seared duck breast in this menu.

In a large saucepan over medium-high heat, melt the butter. Add the turnip and carrot and sauté until lightly browned, about 7 minutes. Add the cabbage and sauté until wilted, about 2 minutes. Stir in the broth, reduce the heat to medium-low, and cook, uncovered, until the cabbage is tender and most of the cooking liquid has evaporated, about 10 minutes.

Season to taste with salt and pepper and stir in the parsley. Serve at once.

Each recipe serves 6

Pear, Endive, and Walnut Salad

Asian pears are a particularly good choice for salads, as they remain crisp when tossed with a vinaigrette. Their aromatic character pairs well with the tartness of a young, soft goat cheese and the richness of a creamy blue, making them a good match for this menu's cheese course.

In a large bowl, combine the pear slices and lemon juice, and toss to coat the pear slices evenly to keep them from turning brown.

In a small bowl, whisk together the vinegar, mustard, and shallot. Slowly stream in the olive oil while whisking constantly to make a vinaigrette. Continue to whisk until emulsified. Season to taste with salt and pepper.

In a small, dry frying pan over medium heat, toast the nuts, shaking the pan often, until they start to brown and smell aromatic, about 7 minutes. Transfer to a small dish and set aside.

Add the endive to the bowl holding the pears. Drizzle with the vinaigrette, then toss to coat evenly. Divide the salad evenly among salad plates. Top each serving with an equal number of walnut halves. Serve at once.

3 Asian or Bosc pears, halved, cored, and cut into slices 1/8 inch (3 mm) thick

Juice of 1 lemon

3 tablespoons sherry vinegar

1 teaspoon Dijon mustard

1 shallot, minced

1/2 cup (4 fl oz/125 ml) extra-virgin olive oil

Coarse salt and freshly ground pepper

1/2 cup (2 oz/60 g) walnut halves

3 large heads Belgian endive (chicory/witloof), cored and cut lengthwise into narrow strips

Selection of Artisanal Cheeses

An artisanal cheese is any cheese that has been both made and ripened naturally. Look for a well-stocked cheese shop with a knowledgeable staff to guide you. For a table of six guests, select three cheeses of differing ages and styles.

About 2 hours before serving, remove the cheeses from the refrigerator, unwrap them, and allow them to come to room temperature.

When ready to serve, line a wooden cheese board with the leaves and arrange the cheeses on it. Serve the bread in a basket alongside the board.

Each recipe serves 6

6–8 oz (185–250 g) ash-coated goat cheese such as Valençay, Humbolt Fog, or Selles-sur-Cher

6–8 oz (185–250 g) semifirm cow's-milk cheese such as Saint George, Carmody, or Gruyère

6–8 oz (185–250 g) blue-veined cheese such as Saint-Agur, fourme d'ambert, or dolcelatte Gorgonzola

Pesticide-free grapevine or fig leaves for serving

Nut bread

4 oranges

12 tablespoons (6 oz/185 g) firmly packed golden brown sugar

6 tablespoons (3 oz/90 g) unsalted butter, melted, plus ¹/₂ cup (4 oz/125 g) unsalted butter, at room temperature

¹/₂ cup (4 oz/125 g) granulated sugar

Grated zest of 1 orange

2 eggs

1 cup (5 oz/155 g) all-purpose (plain) flour

1 teaspoon baking powder

¹/₂ teaspoon baking soda (bicarbonate of soda)

¹/₄ teaspoon salt

¹/₄ cup (2 fl oz/60 ml) heavy (double) cream

1 teaspoon vanilla extract (essence)

Crème Anglaise (page 273)

INDIVIDUAL ORANGE BUTTER CAKES

With the mellow flavor and delicate scent of apricots, and a light almond aftertaste, orange Muscats complement many fruit desserts, among them these individual cakes made from fresh orange segments.

Preheat the oven to 350°F (180°C). Lightly butter six 1-cup (8–fl oz/250-ml) ramekins or custard cups.

Working with 1 orange at a time, and using a sharp knife, cut a slice off both ends of the orange to reveal the flesh. Stand the orange upright on a cutting board and, using the knife, thickly slice off the peel and pith in strips, following the contour of the fruit. Holding the orange in one hand, cut along either side of each section to release it from the membrane, letting the sections drop into a bowl.

Sprinkle 2 tablespoons of the brown sugar in the bottom of each prepared ramekin. Pour 1 tablespoon of the melted butter into each ramekin, evenly covering the sugar. Divide the orange sections evenly among the ramekins, placing them in a single layer. Place the ramekins on a rimmed baking sheet.

Using an electric mixer on medium-high speed, beat together the ¹/₂ cup butter, the granulated sugar, and the orange zest until creamy. Add the eggs one at a time, beating well after each addition. In a bowl, sift together the flour, baking powder, baking soda, and salt. Using a rubber spatula, fold the flour mixture into the butter mixture. Stir in the cream and vanilla extract until thoroughly incorporated. Spoon the batter over the oranges, dividing it evenly among the ramekins.

Bake until the tops are golden and a toothpick inserted into the center of a cake comes out clean, about 35 minutes. Remove from the oven, transfer the cakes to a wire rack, and let them cool for 10 minutes.

Run a knife blade around the edge of each cake to loosen it from the ramekin. Working with 1 cake at a time, invert a small dessert plate over the ramekin, then invert the ramekin and plate in a single quick motion. Lightly tap the bottom of the ramekin with the handle of the knife to loosen the cake, then lift off the ramekin. If any orange sections stick to the ramekins, use a knife tip to loosen them and replace them on the cakes. Serve the cakes warm or at room temperature with the crème anglaise poured over the top.

Serves 6

THANKSGIVING FEAST

At this homey family gathering, Thanksgiving takes on a lighter, more contemporary feel without losing any of its traditional delights. A wooden farm table with benches holds a crowd and sets a cozy, welcoming mood. The meal is served buffet style, but the table is laid with full place settings and decorated in rich autumnal tones.

Woven place mats and a simple arrangement of seasonal fruits in a rustic wooden bowl, in place of a tablecloth and flowers, add to the natural warmth of the setting. Linen napkins are given a simple fold and a sprig of bay for color and fragrance.

MENU

*Carrot Soup with Bacon
and Chestnut Cream*

Sage-Rubbed Turkey

Bread and Sausage Stuffing

Pear and Cranberry Chutney

Sweet Potato Purée

Green Beans with Almonds

Barley Pilaf with Chanterelles

Pumpkin Pie with Candied Pecans

Chardonnay

TIPS FOR HOLIDAY BUFFETS

- Be sure your place at the table is near the kitchen for easy access.

- Do not be afraid to mix heirloom platters with modern pieces, as long as the colors are complementary.

- Serve kids drinks—sparkling cider, grape juice, or even water—in wine-glasses to mark the special occasion.

WORK PLAN

AT LEAST ONE DAY IN ADVANCE

Coat the turkey with the rub

Boil the green beans

Make the chutney

Candy the pecans for the pie

THE DAY OF THE PARTY

Make the soup and chestnut cream

Cook and cool the stuffing

Roast the turkey

Bake the pie

JUST BEFORE SERVING

Reheat the soup

Make the gravy

Make the sweet potato dish

Sauté the green beans

Make the barley pilaf

line kraft-paper boxes, which can be found at art supply or restaurant supply stores—or ask a favorite restaurant to sell you a few—with sheets of parchment (baking) or waxed paper.

tie each box with a pretty ribbon and tuck a fresh herb sprig, such as sage, rosemary, or bay, under the bow.

pack each box with slices of turkey slipped into a zippered plastic bag, then in colored tissue or parchment, along with a small container filled with stuffing and cranberry relish.

attach a gift tag or label that describes what is inside, or conveys a simple, personal Thanksgiving message.

NEXT-DAY TURKEY SANDWICH KIT

On the day after Thanksgiving, indulging in a turkey sandwich is a ritual almost as beloved as the holiday dinner itself. With a little preparation, you can turn the meal's leftovers into thoughtful gifts for your guests to take home to enjoy.

Carrot Soup with Bacon and Chestnut Cream

For convenience, look for vacuum-packed chestnuts sold in jars or plastic pouches. The hard outer shells and bitter inner skins have already been peeled away, saving you considerable preparation time. Avoid chestnuts packed in water in cans; they have poor texture and lack flavor.

In a large saucepan over medium heat, fry the bacon until crisp, about 6 minutes. Using a slotted spoon, transfer the bacon to paper towels to drain. When cool, crumble the bacon and set aside.

Pour off the bacon fat from the pan, return the pan to medium heat, and add the butter. When the butter has melted, add the onion and leek and sauté until golden, about 10 minutes. Add the carrots, potato, and 6 cups of the broth and bring to a boil over high heat. Reduce the heat to low, cover partially, and simmer until all the vegetables are tender, about 45 minutes.

Meanwhile, make the chestnut cream: In a small saucepan over low heat, combine the chestnuts and broth. Cover and cook until the chestnuts are tender, about 15 minutes. Remove from the heat and transfer the contents of the pan to a blender. Add the crème fraîche and a pinch of nutmeg and process until smooth. Transfer to a small bowl and set aside until serving. (The cream can be made up to 24 hours in advance, covered, and refrigerated; bring to room temperature before serving.)

When the vegetables are done, remove from the heat and process with an immersion blender until smooth, or process in a stand blender in batches, then return the soup to the saucepan. If the soup is too thick, add broth as needed to thin to a good consistency. Season to taste with salt and pepper. (You can make the soup up to this point, let cool, cover, and refrigerate for up to 24 hours. When ready to serve, reheat gently, thinning the soup with more broth if necessary.)

Reheat the soup to serving temperature over low heat. Ladle into warmed bowls and top each serving with a swirl of the chestnut cream and a sprinkle each with the chives and bacon. Serve at once.

Serves 8–10

4 slices bacon

4 tablespoons (2 oz/60 g) unsalted butter

1 yellow onion, chopped

1 leek, including tender green tops, chopped

2 lb (1 kg) carrots, peeled and thinly sliced

1 russet potato, peeled and diced

6–8 cups (48–64 fl oz/1.5–2 l) reduced-sodium chicken broth

CHESTNUT CREAM

1/2 cup (2 oz/60 g) vacuum-packed chestnuts

1/4 cup (2 fl oz/60 ml) reduced-sodium chicken broth

1/3 cup (3 oz/90 g) crème fraîche

Freshly grated nutmeg

Coarse salt and freshly ground pepper

2 tablespoons finely snipped fresh chives

SAGE-RUBBED TURKEY

2 tablespoons coarse salt

2 teaspoons freshly ground pepper

1 teaspoon ground sage

2 tablespoons chopped fresh sage

4 cloves garlic, chopped

Grated zest of 1 lemon

1 turkey, about 12 lb (6 kg), rinsed inside and out and patted dry with paper towels

Bread and Sausage Stuffing (page 231)

1 carrot, peeled and cut into 1-inch (2.5-cm) pieces

1 celery stalk, cut into 1-inch (2.5-cm) pieces

1 yellow onion, cut into 1-inch (2.5-cm) cubes

2 cups (16 fl oz/500 ml) dry white wine

2 cups (16 fl oz/500 ml) reduced-sodium chicken broth

3 tablespoons all-purpose (plain) flour

Coarse salt and freshly ground pepper

For a moist, flavorful bird, always start with a fresh free-range turkey. When you carve the bird, arrange the white and dark meat separately so that guests will easily be able to find the cut they prefer at the buffet.

To make the sage rub, in a spice grinder, combine the salt, pepper, ground sage, chopped sage, garlic, and lemon zest and grind until fine. Rub the sage mixture evenly over the skin and inside both cavities of the turkey. Place the bird on a baking sheet, cover lightly with plastic wrap, and refrigerate for 24 hours.

Remove the turkey from the refrigerator about 1 hour before roasting it. Position a rack in the lower third of the oven and preheat to 425°F (220°C). Pat the turkey dry with paper towels. Loosely stuff the neck and body cavities with the stuffing. Tuck the turkey's wings under to secure the neck skin, then loosely tie the legs together with kitchen string. Scatter the carrot, celery, and onion pieces in a large, heavy roasting pan and add the wine. Place the bird, breast side up, on the vegetables.

Roast the turkey for 45 minutes. Reduce the heat to 350°F (180°C) and continue roasting, basting with the pan juices every 30 minutes, until an instant-read thermometer inserted into the thickest part of the thigh away from bone registers 175°F (80°C), $2^1/_2$–3 hours. Transfer the turkey to a cutting board and tent it with aluminum foil. Allow to rest for 15–20 minutes before carving.

While the turkey is resting, in a small saucepan over medium heat, heat the broth until simmering. Pour the juices from the roasting pan into a heatproof measuring pitcher. Skim off 3 tablespoons of the fat and return it to the pan. Skim off and discard the remaining fat and pour the juices into the simmering broth. Place the roasting pan on the stove top over medium heat. Sprinkle in the flour while stirring continuously with a wooden spoon, scraping up any brown bits on the pan bottom. Stream in the hot broth while whisking constantly to break up any lumps that form. Reduce the heat to low and simmer, stirring occasionally to prevent scorching, until slightly thickened, about 5 minutes. Season to taste with salt and pepper. Pour the gravy through a fine-mesh sieve into a warmed bowl for passing at the table.

Remove the trussing string. Scoop the stuffing out of the cavities into a warmed large bowl. Carve the turkey and arrange the pieces on a warmed platter. Serve at once.

Serves 8–10

BREAD AND SAUSAGE STUFFING

Spoon any extra stuffing into a buttered baking dish and bake it next to the turkey during the last 40 minutes of roasting. While the turkey rests, keep the stuffing in the oven to develop a golden brown crust.

Preheat the oven to 350°F (180°C). Spread the bread cubes on a rimmed baking sheet and toast in the oven until golden, about 20 minutes. Remove from the oven and set aside to cool.

In a large frying pan over medium heat, melt the butter. Add the sausage, onion, leek, celery, and sage and cook, breaking up the meat into small pieces with a wooden spoon, until the meat browns and is cooked through and the vegetables are translucent, about 10 minutes. Remove from the heat and fold in the bread cubes, parsley, and half-and-half. Stir in the broth until the mixture is evenly moistened. Season to taste with salt and pepper. Let cool completely before stuffing into the cavities of the turkey.

1 loaf sourdough French bread, 1 lb (500 g), cut into 1/2-inch (12-mm) cubes

2 tablespoons unsalted butter

1 lb (500 g) sweet Italian sausage, casings removed

1 yellow onion, chopped

1 leek, including tender green tops, chopped

1 celery stalk, chopped

1/4 cup (1/3 oz/10 g) chopped fresh sage

1/2 cup (3/4 oz/20 g) chopped fresh flat-leaf (Italian) parsley

1 cup (8 fl oz/250 ml) half-and-half (half cream)

1 1/2 cups (12 fl oz/375 ml) reduced-sodium chicken broth

Coarse salt and freshly ground pepper

PEAR AND CRANBERRY CHUTNEY

This chutney, which marries flavorful Bosc pears with tart cranberries and an assortment of spices, is roasted in the oven, where it can be left unattended, rather than simmered on the stove top.

Preheat the oven to 350°F (180°C). In a 9-by-13-inch (23-by-33-cm) baking dish, stir together the pears, cranberries, onion, ginger, cinnamon, cardamom, cloves, a pinch of cayenne, the orange zest, butter, and golden brown sugar.

Roast the chutney until the pears are very soft and the cranberries have started to break down, about 2 hours. Remove from the oven, stir in the pear nectar and vinegar, and let cool to room temperature. (The chutney can be stored in an airtight container in the refrigerator for up to 2 weeks.)

Transfer the chutney to a serving bowl and serve.

Each recipe serves 8–10

4 Bosc pears, peeled, cored, and cut into 1/4-inch (6-mm) cubes

3 cups (12 oz/375 g) fresh or frozen cranberries

1 yellow onion, diced

1 tablespoon peeled and grated fresh ginger

1 teaspoon *each* ground cinnamon and ground cardamom

1/4 teaspoon ground cloves

Cayenne pepper

Grated zest of 1 orange

4 tablespoons (2 oz/60 g) unsalted butter, melted

1/2 cup (3 1/2 oz/105 g) firmly packed golden brown sugar

1/4 cup (2 fl oz/60 ml) pear nectar

2 tablespoons cider vinegar

Sweet Potato Purée

4 lb (2 kg) orange-fleshed sweet potatoes, peeled and cut into 1-inch (2.5-cm) cubes

Coarse salt

1¼ cups (10 fl oz/310 ml) half-and-half (half cream)

¼ cup (2¾ fl oz/85 ml) maple syrup

5 tablespoons (2½ oz/75 g) unsalted butter

Freshly ground white pepper

Look for sweet potatoes that have dark brownish orange skin and a bright orange interior, sometimes labeled "yams" at the supermarket. Their flesh is naturally moist and sweet when cooked and puréed.

In a large saucepan over medium heat, combine the sweet potatoes, 2 teaspoons salt, and water to cover by 2 inches (5 cm). Bring to a boil and cook until tender when pierced with a knife, about 20 minutes. Drain into a colander and transfer to a large bowl. Using a potato masher, mash the sweet potatoes thoroughly.

In a small saucepan over medium heat, warm the half-and-half and maple syrup until hot. Remove from the heat. Add 4 tablespoons (2 oz/60 g) of the butter to the sweet potatoes, then slowly pour in the hot half-and-half mixture while stirring with a wooden spoon. Continue to stir the potatoes until they are light and creamy. Season to taste with salt and white pepper. Transfer the sweet potatoes to a warmed serving bowl and top with the remaining 1 tablespoon butter. Serve at once.

Green Beans with Almonds

Coarse salt

2 lb (1 kg) slender green beans, trimmed

½ cup (2½ oz/75 g) slivered blanched almonds

2 tablespoons unsalted butter

1 tablespoon olive oil

4 shallots, thinly sliced

Freshly ground pepper

2 tablespoons chopped fresh flat-leaf (Italian) parsley

These simply prepared beans put a touch of bright color on an autumn buffet. Look for young Blue Lake beans or slender French haricots verts.

Fill a large pot three-fourths full of lightly salted water and bring to a boil over high heat. Add the beans. Cook the beans until tender, about 5 minutes. Drain into a colander, refresh with cold water, and pat dry with paper towels. Set aside. (The beans can be prepared up to this point 1 day in advance, covered tightly, and refrigerated until needed.)

In a large frying pan over medium heat, toast the almonds, stirring continuously, until golden brown, about 3 minutes. Transfer to a plate and set aside. In the same pan over medium heat, melt the butter with the olive oil. Add the shallots and sauté until translucent and beginning to brown, 4–5 minutes. Raise the heat to medium-high and stir in the beans. Sauté, stirring continuously, until heated through and beginning to brown, about 4 minutes. Season with salt and pepper and stir in the parsley and almonds. Transfer to a warmed serving bowl and serve at once.

Each recipe serves 8–10

Barley Pilaf with Chanterelles

Flavorful pearl barley replaces the usual rice in this quick and easy pilaf. Chanterelles are called for here, but other seasonal wild or cultivated mushrooms can be used as well, such as porcini (ceps), morels, shiitakes, or oyster mushrooms.

In a large saucepan over medium heat, melt the butter. Add the leek and sauté until translucent, about 4 minutes. Raise the heat to medium-high, add the chanterelles, and cook, stirring, until soft, about 3 minutes.

Add the thyme and barley and stir to coat the grains with the butter. Pour in the wine and cook until absorbed, about 1 minute. Add the broth, bring to a boil, reduce the heat to low, cover, and cook until the liquid has been absorbed and the barley is tender, about 13 minutes. Remove from the heat and let stand for 5 minutes to marry the flavors.

Season the barley to taste with salt and pepper, transfer to a warmed serving bowl, and serve at once.

Serves 8–10

4 tablespoons (2 oz/60 g) unsalted butter

1 leek, including tender green tops, finely chopped

1/2 lb (250 g) fresh chanterelle mushrooms, brushed clean and sliced lengthwise

2 tablespoons finely chopped fresh thyme

2 1/2 cups (17 1/2 oz/545 g) quick-cooking pearl barley

1 cup (8 fl oz/250 ml) dry white wine

2 1/2 cups (20 fl oz/625 ml) reduced-sodium chicken broth, heated

Coarse salt and freshly ground pepper

PUMPKIN PIE WITH CANDIED PECANS

Candied pecans are used to flavor a graham cracker crumb crust in this otherwise classic pumpkin pie seasoned with clove, cinnamon, and ginger. You will not need all of the candied pecans for this recipe, but the remainder are delicious chopped and sprinkled on vanilla ice cream.

Preheat the oven to 350°F (180°C). Lightly oil a rimmed baking sheet. To make the candied pecans, sift together the superfine sugar, cinnamon, and nutmeg onto a plate. Place the pecans in a colander and rinse under running cold water. Shake the colander to remove the excess water and toss the pecans in the sugar mixture, coating them evenly. Spread the nuts out on the prepared baking sheet in a single layer, separating any that are touching.

Bake the nuts until they are dry and the sugar has crystallized, about 25 minutes. Remove from the oven and let cool completely. Store in an airtight container at room temperature until needed, or for up to 2 days.

To make the crust, measure out 1 cup of the candied pecans, place in a food processor, and process until finely ground. Pour into a bowl and stir in the graham cracker crumbs and butter until all the ingredients are evenly moistened. Pour into a 9-inch (23-cm) pie dish and, using your fingers, press the mixture to cover the bottom and sides of the dish evenly. Set aside.

Preheat the oven to 325°F (165°C).

To make the filling, whisk together the pumpkin purée, eggs, cream, brown sugar, cornstarch, cinnamon, ginger, nutmeg, cloves, and vanilla extract until well combined. Pour the mixture into the prepared crust and smooth the top.

Bake the pie until a toothpick or thin skewer inserted into the center comes out clean, 50–60 minutes. Transfer to a wire rack and let cool completely.

Just before serving, garnish the edge of the pie with some of the candied pecan halves. Cut the pie into wedges and place a slice on each plate. Top each serving with a spoonful of whipped cream. Sprinkle the whipped cream with a little nutmeg. Serve at once.

Serves 8–10

CANDIED PECANS

1/3 cup (2 1/2 oz/75 g) superfine (caster) sugar

1 teaspoon ground cinnamon

1/4 teaspoon freshly grated nutmeg

2 cups (8 oz/250 g) pecan halves

CRUST

1 cup (4 oz/125 g) candied pecans

1 cup (3 oz/90 g) fine cinnamon graham cracker crumbs

1/2 cup (4 oz/125 g) unsalted butter, melted

FILLING

1 can (15 oz/470 g) pumpkin purée

3 large eggs, lightly beaten

3/4 cup (6 fl oz/180 ml) heavy (double) cream

2/3 cup (5 oz/155 g) firmly packed dark brown sugar

1 tablespoon cornstarch (cornflour)

1 teaspoon ground cinnamon

1 teaspoon ground ginger

1/4 teaspoon freshly grated nutmeg

1/4 teaspoon ground cloves

1 teaspoon vanilla extract (essence)

Sweetened whipped cream and freshly grated nutmeg for serving

WINTER

MENUS FOR WINTER

WEEKEND BREAKFAST

Oatmeal Pancakes

Cheddar and Vegetable Frittata

Apple and Sausage Patties

Apple Wood–Smoked Bacon

242

TRADITIONAL CHRISTMAS DINNER

Oyster Stew

Standing Rib Roast with Madeira Jus

Yorkshire Puddings

Herbed Horseradish Sauce

Potato and Celery Root Purée

Creamed Spinach

*Bread Puddings with Dried Fruit
and Crème Anglaise*

256

NEW YEAR'S EVE
COCKTAIL PARTY

Cranberry Cocktails

Oysters with Mignonette Sauce

Traditional Caviar Service

Smoked Salmon Pinwheels

Lemongrass Shrimp Skewers

Tuna Tartare on Flat Bread

Beef Tenderloin Canapés

Fruit Tartlets

274

VALENTINE'S DAY DINNER
FOR TWO

Champagne

*Crab, Avocado, and Grapefruit Salad
with Chive Vinaigrette*

Pink Peppercorn Rack of Lamb

Roasted Yukon Gold Potatoes

Chocolate Crème Brûlée

294

WEEKEND BREAKFAST

A hearty midwinter breakfast for friends provides a novel departure from the usual evening parties of the season. As morning light filters through the windows, guests gather in the warmth of the kitchen over steamy mugs of hot chocolate, while the host puts the finishing touches on the

food. Arranged on a countertop beside the kitchen table, the abundant buffet features traditional morning favorites. Herb topiaries add a bright splash of green, and bowls of colorful winter fruits take the place of floral arrangements to round out the simple, homey tablesetting.

TIPS FOR MEMORABLE BREAKFASTS

- Spike hot chocolate with half the volume of coffee; garnish it with whipped cream and shaved chocolate.

- In winter, citrus season, squeeze an assortment of fresh juices for the table.

- Alter the menu for any season by changing the vegetable or fruit components of the meal.

MENU

Blood Orange Juice and
Hot Chocolate

Oatmeal Pancakes

Cheddar and Vegetable Frittata

Apple and Sausage Patties

Apple Wood–Smoked Bacon

WORK PLAN

AT LEAST ONE DAY IN ADVANCE
Mix the cinnamon butter

Prepare the sausage mixture

THE DAY OF THE PARTY
Make the frittata

JUST BEFORE SERVING
Cook the pancakes and set out the toppings

Panfry the sausage patties and bacon slices

TILE FOOD WARMERS

Unless you have a hot plate or chafing dish, keeping buffet food warm can be a challenge. Heating oversized tiles in the oven and placing them under the serving platters, on an insulating material, is a stylish solution that helps unify the look of the buffet.

heat large ceramic or terra-cotta tiles (available at ceramic wholesalers or building-supply stores) in a 250°F (120°C) oven until they are hot, about 20 minutes. Be sure to use a thick pot holder when moving them.

position the tiles on the insulating material just before you are ready to set out the food, spacing them at intervals to accommodate all of the platters.

cover the buffet surface with a thick, heat-resistant material, or fold a thick tablecloth several times to form a long runner. This will protect the finish of the furniture and help keep the heat from dissipating.

place the warmed platters of food on top of the hot tiles. Remember to set the appropriate utensils alongside the platters for serving.

Oatmeal Pancakes

Rolled oats and buttermilk flavor these pancakes, which are a nice twist on the original. Other fresh and dried fruits and toasted nuts can be offered in place of what is suggested here. Sliced strawberries, chopped dried apples, and almonds, for example, are a good combination.

To make the cinnamon butter, in a small bowl, using a wooden spoon, mix together the butter and cinnamon until the cinnamon is evenly distributed. Place the mixture on a piece of waxed paper and fold the paper over to cover the butter. Roll the butter back and forth inside the paper to form a log about 3 inches (7.5 cm) long by 1 inch (2.5 cm) in diameter. Twist the ends of the paper and place the log in the freezer for 10 minutes to harden, or refrigerate for up to 24 hours.

To make the pancakes, in a large mixing bowl, whisk together the all-purpose flour, cake flour, oats, sugar, baking powder, baking soda, and salt. In a separate bowl, whisk together the eggs, buttermilk, and 5 tablespoons melted butter until well combined. Add the egg mixture to the dry ingredients and whisk until combined. Let the batter rest at room temperature for 10 minutes.

Preheat the oven to 200°F (95°C).

Heat a nonstick frying pan or griddle over medium-high heat and brush lightly with butter. To form each pancake, fill a measuring pitcher with ⅓ cup (3 fl oz/80 ml) of the batter and pour it onto the heated surface. It will spread into a round about 5 inches (13 cm) in diameter. Be careful not to crowd the pan. Cook until the edges are set and bubbles appear in the center of the pancake, about 2 minutes. Using a spatula, carefully flip the pancakes and cook on the other side until golden, about 1 minute longer. Transfer the pancakes to a rimmed baking sheet and keep warm in the oven. Repeat until all the batter is used.

To serve, put the walnuts, bananas, and currants in separate small serving bowls. Pour the maple syrup into a warmed pitcher. Cut the cinnamon butter into slices ¼ inch (6 mm) thick and arrange on a small plate or saucer. Place all the toppings on the table. Transfer the pancakes to a warmed serving platter and place on the table. Let each guest build and top his or her own stack of pancakes.

Serves 6

CINNAMON BUTTER

½ cup (4 oz/125 g) unsalted butter, at room temperature

2 teaspoons ground cinnamon

PANCAKES

1 cup (5 oz/155 g) all-purpose (plain) flour

½ cup (2 oz/60 g) cake (soft-wheat) flour

½ cup (1½ oz/45 g) quick-cooking rolled oats

3 tablespoons sugar

2 teaspoons baking powder

1 teaspoon baking soda (bicarbonate of soda)

¼ teaspoon salt

2 large eggs

2½ cups (20 fl oz/625 ml) buttermilk

5 tablespoons (2½ oz/75 g) unsalted butter, melted, plus more for cooking

TOPPINGS

1 cup (4 oz/125 g) walnut pieces, toasted (page 215) and chopped

2 bananas, peeled and thinly sliced

½ cup (3 oz/90 g) dried currants

2 cups (22 fl oz/690 ml) maple syrup, heated

CHEDDAR AND VEGETABLE FRITTATA

Frittatas, which are large, flat (rather than folded) Italian omelets, can be made with nearly any combination of vegetables, cheeses, and cured or cooked meats. Another complementary cheese, such as dry jack or Asiago, could be used in place of the crumbly aged Cheddar.

Position a rack in the upper third of the oven and preheat to 450°F (230°C).

In a bowl, whisk together the eggs, cheese, and parsley just until blended. Set aside.

In an ovenproof, nonstick 9-inch (23-cm) frying pan over medium-high heat, melt the butter with the olive oil. Add the green onions and zucchini and sauté until tender and lightly golden, about 5 minutes. Season the vegetables to taste with salt and pepper and spread them in an even layer on the pan bottom. Pour the egg mixture over the vegetables, being careful not to dislodge them. Reduce the heat to low and cook until the egg begins to set and the sides of the frittata start to brown, about 5 minutes. Place the pan in the oven and cook until the frittata is firm to touch and the top is golden, about 5 minutes longer.

Remove the frittata from the oven and let cool slightly. Cut into wedges and serve directly from the pan or transfer the wedges to a serving platter. Serve warm or at room temperature.

Serves 6

4 large eggs

1 cup (4 oz/125 g) finely shredded extra-sharp Cheddar cheese

2 tablespoons chopped fresh flat-leaf (Italian) parsley

2 tablespoons unsalted butter

2 tablespoons olive oil

4 green (spring) onions, including tender green tops, chopped

3/4 lb (375 g) zucchini (courgettes), trimmed and thinly sliced

Coarse salt and freshly ground pepper

Apple and Sausage Patties

Adding grated apple to bulk pork sausage yields tangy, flavorful breakfast patties. Easy to make, they are a nice alternative to ready-made sausages and are an interesting addition to a breakfast buffet.

In a bowl, combine the sausage, apple, bread crumbs, cream, and egg yolk and mix until well combined. Mix in $1/2$ teaspoon salt and $1/4$ teaspoon pepper. Divide the mixture into 12 equal portions and shape each portion into a patty 2 inches (5 cm) in diameter and $1/4$ inch (6 mm) thick. Arrange the patties on a rimmed baking sheet or tray and refrigerate for 15 minutes, or cover tightly with plastic wrap and refrigerate overnight. Bring to room temperature before cooking.

Preheat the oven to 200°F (95°C). Place a large frying pan over medium-low heat and lightly brush it with canola oil. Place 4 of the patties in the pan and fry until browned on one side, about 3 minutes. Carefully flip each of the patties and fry until browned on the second side and cooked through, about 4 minutes longer. Transfer the patties to an ovenproof dish and keep warm in the oven. Cook the remaining patties in the same way, oiling the pan between batches. Keep warm until ready to serve. Arrange the patties on a serving platter and serve at once.

1 lb (500 g) bulk pork sausage

1 tart green apple, peeled, cored, and grated

$1/4$ cup (1 oz/30 g) fine dried bread crumbs

2 tablespoons heavy (double) cream

1 large egg yolk

Coarse salt and freshly ground pepper

Canola oil for cooking

Apple Wood–Smoked Bacon

Everyone will know it is breakfast time when the smoky-sweet aroma of apple wood bacon fills the air. Look for bacon that is thick sliced and preferably cured without nitrates. Start the bacon in a cold frying pan; the slices will shrink less and splattering will be reduced.

Lay the bacon slices in a single layer in 2 large, cold frying pans, being careful not to crowd them. Place the pans over medium heat and cook until the edges of the slices start to curl and the bacon starts to brown, about 3 minutes. Using kitchen tongs, turn the bacon slices over and cook until browned, about 3 minutes longer. Transfer the slices to a plate lined with paper towels to drain briefly, then transfer to a serving platter and serve at once.

Each recipe serves 6

1 lb (500 g) thick-sliced apple wood–smoked bacon

TRADITIONAL CHRISTMAS DINNER

A classic English Christmas feast brings friends and family together for an unforgettable celebration. The good china comes out of the cupboard, the silver is polished, and the dining room takes on a look of jewel-toned opulence. The table is set with deep red and purple linens, twinkling votive candles, and individual floral arrangements. Ruby

glass cordial cups hold snow white tulips, red berries, and pine sprigs. Around the room, the decor is kept simple so as not to distract from the beauty of the table. The sumptuous menu matches the setting, with big, rich flavors that reflect the bountiful spirit of the holiday.

WORK PLAN

AT LEAST ONE DAY IN ADVANCE

Mix the herbed horseradish sauce

Make the crème anglaise for the
bread puddings

THE DAY OF THE PARTY

Coat the roast with the spice paste

Mix the Yorkshire pudding batter

Roast the beef

Soak the bread pudding mixture

JUST BEFORE SERVING

Make the oyster stew

Bake the Yorkshire puddings

Prepare the spinach

Make the potato and celery root dish

Bake the bread puddings

MENU

Oyster Stew

Standing Rib Roast with Madeira Jus

Yorkshire Puddings

Herbed Horseradish Sauce

Potato and Celery Root Purée

Creamed Spinach

*Bread Puddings with Dried Fruit
and Crème Anglaise*

Cabernet Sauvignon

TIPS FOR WINTER
HOLIDAY DINNERS

- Decorate the mantel with freshly cut pine boughs and white candles in different heights.

- Make centerpieces for the table by filling footed glass bowls with seasonal fruits and holiday ornaments.

- At the table, seat kids between adults for a lively mix of ages.

- Place a whimsical gift or creative name card at each place setting.

WINTRY FLORAL SATELLITES

A repeating floral motif is a good way to bring a festive table together. Here, each guest is given his or her own focal point of decorative color—cheerful, wintry red, white, and green—keeping the sight lines clear.

gather everything you will need: white tulips, stems of red berries, pine or other greenery sprigs, small glasses or bud vases, pruning shears, and a pitcher of water.

trim the stems of the flowers, berries, and greenery so that 2 to 4 inches (5 to 10 cm) will be exposed when they are placed in the glasses. Vary the lengths to add visual interest.

arrange the elements in the glasses filled halfway with water, starting with the flowers and then tucking in the berries and greenery to make a pleasing, natural-looking cluster.

OYSTER STEW

Oyster stew is a New England classic and a natural first course for an old-fashioned standing rib roast Christmas dinner. If you are rushed, look for freshly shucked oysters packed in their own liquor. They are sold in jars at most fish markets.

Scrub the oysters with a stiff brush, then rinse well under running cold water. Working with 1 oyster at a time, use a thick folded cloth to hold the oyster in one hand, with the flat top shell facing up. Using an oyster knife in the other hand, insert its tip between the shells near the hinge of the oyster. Twist the knife—it may take a bit of strength—to break the hinge. Run the knife along the inside surface of the top shell to loosen the oyster from it. Lift off and discard the top shell. Drain the liquor from the bottom shell into a bowl. Run the knife along the inside surface of the bottom shell to sever the muscle that attaches the shell to the oyster, and place the oyster in a separate bowl. Repeat with the remaining oysters. Set the oyster liquor and oysters aside.

In a large saucepan over medium heat, melt the butter. Add the green onions and sauté until soft, about 3 minutes. Pour in the vermouth and simmer until almost all the liquid has evaporated, about 3 minutes. Stir in the milk, cream, and reserved oyster liquor and bring to a simmer, stirring constantly. Add the oysters and cook until they are opaque and the edges start to curl, about 3 minutes. Remove from the heat and season to taste with salt.

Ladle the stew into warmed soup bowls and garnish each serving with a grind of black pepper and a sprinkle each of paprika and parsley. Serve at once.

Serves 6

36 oysters in the shell

6 tablespoons (3 oz/90 g) unsalted butter

6 green (spring) onions, including tender green tops, chopped

1/2 cup (4 fl oz/125 ml) dry vermouth

2 cups (16 fl oz/500 ml) whole milk

2 cups (16 fl oz/500 ml) heavy (double) cream

Coarse salt and freshly ground pepper

Sweet Hungarian paprika for garnish

2 tablespoons chopped fresh flat-leaf (Italian) parsley

STANDING RIB ROAST WITH MADEIRA JUS

Seasoned with mustard, rosemary, and thyme and served with a Madeira jus, *this standing rib roast is rich in flavor and classic in its presentation. Ask the butcher to remove the roast's chine bone, to ease carving, and shorten and french the ribs for a nice presentation.*

1 tablespoon olive oil

2 tablespoons Dijon mustard

1 tablespoon chopped fresh thyme

1 tablespoon chopped fresh rosemary

2 cloves garlic, chopped

Coarse salt and freshly ground pepper

1 standing rib roast, about 6–6¹/₂ lb (3–3.25 kg), frenched (see note) with 3 or 4 ribs

MADEIRA JUS

2 cups (16 fl oz/500 ml) dry Madeira

2 tablespoons beef or veal *demi-glace*

In a small bowl, stir together the olive oil, mustard, thyme, rosemary, garlic, 1 tablespoon salt, and 2 teaspoons pepper to form a paste. Smear the paste over the entire roast and let stand at room temperature for 1 hour.

Position a rack in the lower third of the oven and preheat to 450°F (230°C).

Place the roast, bone side down, in a roasting pan and roast for 15 minutes. Reduce the oven temperature to 350°F (180°C) and continue to roast until an instant-read thermometer inserted into the thickest part of the roast away from bone registers 120°F (49°C) for rare and 130°F (54°C) for medium-rare, about 1 hour and 25 minutes longer for rare and 1 hour and 40 minutes longer for medium-rare. Transfer the roast to a warmed serving platter, cover loosely with aluminum foil, and let the meat rest for 15–20 minutes before carving.

Meanwhile, make the Madeira *jus*: Use a large spoon to skim off the fat from the drippings in the roasting pan, and reserve the fat for making the Yorkshire puddings (page 269). Place the roasting pan over medium-high heat and stir the Madeira into the pan juices, scraping up the brown bits from the pan bottom. Whisk in the *demi-glace* and any meat juices that have collected in the bottom of the serving platter. Continue to cook, stirring occasionally, until the liquid is reduced by half, 8–10 minutes longer. Pour the *jus* through a fine-mesh sieve into a warmed serving bowl and skim off any fat that rises to the surface.

Carve the roast tableside—offering the end slices to those who prefer their meat cooked medium and the center slices to those who prefer it more rare—and arrange on warmed individual plates. Pass the *jus* at the table.

Serves 6

Yorkshire Puddings

No Christmas rib roast dinner is complete without these simple savory puddings. The trick to serving Yorkshire puddings that are golden and puffed is timing. They deflate quickly once they are removed from the oven, so you must be prepared to serve them immediately.

In a large bowl, whisk together the flour, thyme, mustard, $1/2$ teaspoon each salt and pepper, eggs, and half-and-half to form a smooth batter. (The batter can be covered and refrigerated for up to 4 hours before continuing.)

Once the roast is removed from the oven, carefully position the rack in the middle, and then raise the temperature to 450°F (230°C). Place an empty 12-cup muffin pan in the oven to heat for 5 minutes. Remove the pan from the oven and brush $1/2$ teaspoon of the rendered beef fat on the bottom and sides of each muffin cup. Remove the batter from the refrigerator and stir lightly if any separation has occurred. Divide the batter evenly among the 12 muffin cups. Bake the puddings until golden and crisp, about 15 minutes. Remove from the oven and, using a table knife, loosen the sides of each pudding to remove them from the pan. Serve the puddings at once while they are still warm and puffed.

1 cup (5 oz/155 g) all-purpose (plain) flour

1 tablespoon chopped fresh thyme

$1/2$ teaspoon dry mustard

Coarse salt and freshly ground pepper

3 large eggs

1 cup (8 fl oz/250 ml) half-and-half (half cream)

6 teaspoons rendered beef fat from the roasting pan (page 266)

Herbed Horseradish Sauce

Roast beef and horseradish sauce are a British pairing of long standing, although the addition of herbs here is a departure from the typical sauce. Other ingredients, such as chopped parsley, sliced green (spring) onions, or capers, can be substituted for the chives, tarragon, and dill.

In a small bowl, stir together the sour cream, horseradish, chives, tarragon, and dill until well combined. (The sauce can be made up to 24 hours in advance and stored, tightly covered, in the refrigerator.)

Transfer the sauce to a small, clear glass serving bowl and serve as a condiment with the roast beef.

Each recipe serves 6

$3/4$ cup (6 oz/180 g) sour cream

$1/4$ cup (2 fl oz/60 ml) prepared horseradish

1 tablespoon snipped fresh chives

1 tablespoon chopped fresh tarragon

1 tablespoon chopped fresh dill

Potato and Celery Root Purée

2 lb (1 kg) Yukon gold potatoes, peeled and cut into 1-inch (2.5-cm) cubes

1 celery root (celeriac), peeled and cut into 1-inch (2.5-cm) pieces

Coarse salt

5 tablespoons (2¹/2 oz/75 g) unsalted butter

¹/4 cup (2 fl oz/60 ml) half-and-half (half cream), heated

2 teaspoons fresh lemon juice

Freshly ground white pepper

Knobby, tough-skinned celery root has a flavor that falls somewhere between celery and parsnip. It imparts a wonderful, aromatic edge when added to a simple dish of puréed potatoes.

In a large saucepan over medium heat, combine the potatoes, celery root, 2 teaspoons salt, and water to cover by 2 inches (5 cm). Bring to a boil and cook until tender when pierced with a knife, about 20 minutes. Drain in a colander, then immediately pass the hot vegetables through a food mill fitted with a medium disk held over a warmed large bowl.

Whisk the butter and half-and-half into the purée. Stir in the lemon juice and season with salt and white pepper. Transfer to a warmed serving bowl and serve at once.

Creamed Spinach

1¹/2 lb (750 g) baby spinach leaves, stems removed

4 tablespoons (2 oz/60 g) unsalted butter

4 green (spring) onions, including tender green tops, chopped

¹/4 cup (1¹/2 oz/45 g) all-purpose (plain) flour

1³/4 cups (14 fl oz/430 ml) half-and-half (half cream), heated

Coarse salt and freshly ground pepper

Freshly grated nutmeg

A rich cream sauce made with half-and-half instead of milk and flavored with sautéed green onions gives this old favorite a new profile. Young spinach has fewer stems and is less bitter than mature leaves.

Bring a large saucepan three-fourths full of water to a boil over high heat. Plunge the spinach leaves into the boiling water and cook for 30 seconds. Pour into a colander, refresh with cold water, and drain well. Squeeze out the excess water from the spinach and chop coarsely. Set aside.

In a large saucepan over medium heat, melt the butter. Add the green onions and sauté for 2 minutes. Sprinkle in the flour while stirring and cook until the mixture is thick and foamy, about 2 minutes. Remove from the heat and slowly stream in the warmed half-and-half while whisking continuously until fully incorporated. Return the pan to low heat, bring to a simmer, and cook, stirring continuously, until thickened, about 3 minutes longer. Stir the prepared spinach into the sauce and season to taste with the salt, pepper, and nutmeg. Transfer to a warmed serving bowl and serve at once.

Each recipe serves 6

BREAD PUDDINGS WITH DRIED FRUIT AND CRÈME ANGLAISE

Egg-rich challah is the starting point for these festive bread puddings. If you are short on time, drizzle each serving with a little heavy cream and warmed store-bought caramel sauce in place of the crème anglaise.

To make the crème anglaise, in a saucepan, whisk together the egg yolks, cornstarch, and the 5 tablespoons sugar until thick and pale yellow, about 2 minutes. Slowly whisk in the hot milk and cream. Add the vanilla bean and place over medium-low heat. Bring to a simmer while stirring continuously with a wooden spoon. Cook, stirring constantly, until thick enough to coat the back of the spoon, about 4 minutes. Remove the vanilla bean halves and, using the tip of a small knife, scrape the seeds from each half into the sauce, then stir to blend. Discard the bean halves. Pour the sauce into a bowl. Cover with plastic wrap, pressing it directly onto the surface to prevent a skin from forming, and refrigerate. (The sauce can be made up to 2 days in advance.)

Lightly butter six 1-cup (8–fl oz/250-ml) ramekins. Coat the bottom and sides with granulated sugar, tapping out the excess. In a large bowl, toss together the bread, figs, dates, ginger, cinnamon, allspice, and melted butter. In a separate bowl, whisk together the whole eggs, egg yolks, and brown sugar until blended and the sugar has dissolved, about 2 minutes. Stir in the half-and-half and vanilla extract. Pour the egg mixture into the bowl holding the bread and dried fruits and toss until well combined. Cover and refrigerate until most of the liquid is absorbed, about 1 hour.

Preheat the oven to 350°F (180°C). Divide the bread pudding mixture evenly among the prepared ramekins. Bake the puddings until the tops are golden and a toothpick inserted into the center of a pudding comes out clean, about 35 minutes. Transfer the puddings to a wire rack and let cool for 15 minutes.

Run a thin-bladed knife around the edge of each mold to loosen the sides of the pudding. The molds may still be too warm to touch, so use a kitchen towel to prevent burning your hands. Working with 1 pudding at a time, remove it from the ramekin and place it standing upright on a dessert plate. Ladle a little of the crème anglaise over the top of each pudding and serve at once.

Serves 6

CRÈME ANGLAISE

2 large egg yolks

2 tablespoons cornstarch (cornflour)

5 tablespoons (2½ oz/75 g) granulated sugar

1 cup (8 fl oz/250 ml) whole milk, heated

1 cup (8 fl oz/250 ml) heavy (double) cream, heated

1 vanilla bean, split lengthwise

Granulated sugar

1 loaf challah, 1 lb (500 g), crust removed and bread torn into bite-sized pieces

1 cup (5 oz/155 g) finely chopped dried figs

1 cup (6 oz/185 g) finely chopped pitted dates

¼ cup (1½ oz/45 g) finely minced crystallized ginger

1 teaspoon ground cinnamon

¼ teaspoon ground allspice

4 tablespoons (2 oz/60 g) unsalted butter, melted

5 large whole eggs, plus 2 large egg yolks

1 cup (7 oz/220 g) firmly packed dark brown sugar

3 cups (24 fl oz/750 ml) half-and-half (half cream)

2 teaspoons vanilla extract (essence)

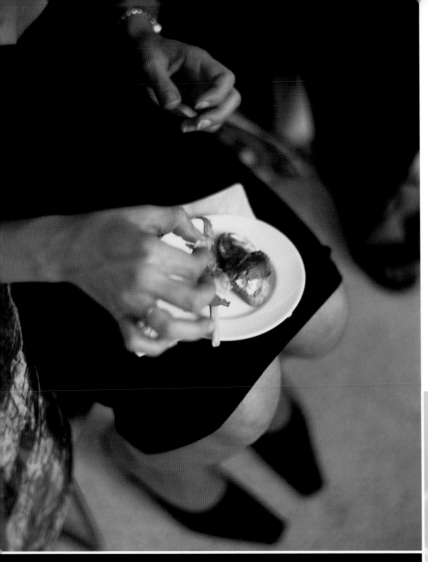

NEW YEAR'S EVE COCKTAIL PARTY

A candlelit cocktail party with a modern mood rings in the New Year in high style. Traditional caviar service and freshly shucked oysters anchor the menu, setting the tone for the ice blue, white, and silver platters that showcase the light, flavorful cocktail food. Dramatic, vertical

arrangements of slender orchids and white calla lilies create a look of minimalist refinement. Illumination comes from candles, a fire in the fireplace, and small lights on the adjacent deck. Cranberry cocktails in martini glasses bring a cool splash of color to the midnight toast.

WORK PLAN

AT LEAST ONE DAY IN ADVANCE

Make the crepes for the
salmon pinwheels

Marinate the shrimp and thread
onto lemongrass skewers

Sear the beef, make the horseradish cream,
and toast the bread for the canapés

THE DAY OF THE PARTY

Make the *mignonette* sauce for the oysters

Assemble the salmon pinwheels

Mix the tuna tartare

JUST BEFORE SERVING

Prepare the caviar accompaniments

Shuck the oysters

Slice the salmon pinwheels

Roast the shrimp skewers

Spoon the tuna tartare onto the flat bread

Assemble the canapés

Put together the tartlets

MENU

Cranberry Cocktails

Oysters with Mignonette Sauce

Traditional Caviar Service

Smoked Salmon Pinwheels

Lemongrass Shrimp Skewers

Tuna Tartare on Flat Bread

Beef Tenderloin Canapés

Fruit Tartlets

TIPS FOR COCKTAIL PARTIES

- Place small bowls of spiced nuts on side tables throughout the room.

- Select food that is comfortable to eat standing up and not too messy.

- Before the party, load the CD player with an assortment of lively music and set it on "shuffle" mode.

- Offer a special cocktail or two, then supplement the offerings with a well-stocked self-serve bar (page 13).

- Enlist a friend or hire a server to help pass the hors d'oeuvres and replenish cocktails.

FESTIVE
INVITATIONS

A party invitation need not be formal or expensively printed. What is most important is to capture the spirit of the festivities. These sparkly black, white, and silver invitations convey the perfect mix of style and fun for New Year's Eve.

write invitations by hand on metallic tags, using both sides. Include the theme of the party, date, time, address, and an RSVP phone number or e-mail address.

stuff the invitations into silver mailing tubes (available at packaging or stationery stores). Add metallic star confetti, foil-wrapped chocolates, or decorative silver wrapping wire, if desired.

attach the tags to hemstitched cocktail napkins—or other items that evoke the theme, such as a party horn or a cocktail stirrer—using silver cord.

affix vintage-style mailing labels, including your return address, and an elegant stamp. Seal the ends of each tube securely. Check with postal authorities to confirm the correct amount of postage.

fill a cocktail shaker half full with ice cubes. Add the liquors and/or juices. Put the lid on the shaker and secure it tightly.

shake vigorously, using an up-and-down motion, for about 10 seconds, to chill and blend the contents thoroughly.

strain the liquid through the perforated lid of the cocktail shaker into chilled martini glasses and finish each drink with the garnish of choice.

CRANBERRY COCKTAILS

The traditional martini is given a holiday hue with a splash of cranberry juice. Cranberry is also featured in a nonalcoholic version of the cosmopolitan, replacing the usual vodka with fresh tangerine juice.

CRANBERRY MARTINIS

Ice cubes

1 cup (8 fl oz/250 ml) vodka

1/4 cup (2 fl oz/60 ml) dry vermouth

1/2 cup (4 fl oz/125 ml) cranberry juice

8 cranberries, frozen

4 lemon zest twists

VIRGIN COSMOPOLITANS

Ice cubes

1 cup (8 fl oz/250 ml) cranberry juice

1 cup (8 fl oz/250 ml) fresh tangerine juice

1/4 cup (2 fl oz/60 ml) fresh lime juice

4 lime zest twists

For the martinis, put 4 martini glasses in the freezer to chill for at least 30 minutes. Just before serving, fill a cocktail shaker half full with ice. Pour over the vodka, vermouth, and cranberry juice. Cover with the lid and shake vigorously up and down for about 10 seconds. Strain into the chilled glasses, dividing evenly. Garnish each glass with 2 frozen cranberries and a lemon twist. Serve at once.

For the cosmopolitans, put 4 martini glasses in the freezer to chill for at least 30 minutes. Just before serving, fill a cocktail shaker half full with ice. Pour over the cranberry juice, tangerine juice, and lime juice. Cover with the lid and shake vigorously up and down for 10 seconds. Strain into the chilled glasses, dividing evenly. Garnish each glass with a lime twist. Serve at once.

Makes 8 cocktails

Oysters with Mignonette Sauce

Chilled mignonette sauce, a classic accompaniment to oysters on the half shell, heightens the flavor of the raw shellfish. Serve a variety of oysters, such as small, sweet Kumamotos, Malapeques, and a local type.

To make the sauce, in a small bowl, stir together the vinegar, lemon juice, and shallot. Season to taste with salt and pepper. Cover and refrigerate until serving.

Scrub the oysters well, then rinse well under running cold water. Cover a large tray with crushed ice. Working with 1 oyster at a time, use a thick folded cloth to hold the oyster in one hand, with the flat top shell facing up. Using an oyster knife in the other hand, insert its tip between the shells near the hinge of the oyster. Twist the knife—it may take a bit of strength—to break the hinge. Run the knife along the inside surface of the top shell to loosen the oyster from it. Lift off and discard the top shell. Run the knife along the inside surface of the bottom shell to sever the muscle that attaches the shell to the oyster. Nest the oyster in its bottom shell in the ice. Repeat with the remaining oysters, arranging them attractively on the ice.

Transfer the sauce to a small serving bowl and place it on the tray with the oysters. Put a stainless-steel or ceramic spoon into the sauce and serve at once.

MIGNONETTE SAUCE

2/3 cup (5 fl oz/160 ml) Champagne vinegar

2 tablespoons fresh lemon juice

2 tablespoons finely chopped shallot

Coarse salt and coarsely ground pepper

20 oysters

Crushed ice

Traditional Caviar Service

The best-known caviars—sevruga, osetra, and beluga—are expensive, but there are several alternative caviars, or roes, which are much less costly and still have good flavor. Make sure the caviar is kept well chilled.

Nest the caviar tin(s) in a bowl of crushed ice and place it on a larger serving tray. Place the egg yolks, egg whites, crème fraîche, and chives in small individual bowls, and arrange them on the tray with the caviar.

Arrange the toasts in a small basket. Place a caviar spoon made of bone, mother of pearl, porcelain, or gold (these materials will not affect the flavor of the caviar) on the tray and allow guests to serve themselves, topping the warm toast squares with caviar and the garnishes of choice.

Each recipe serves 10

6 oz (185 g) caviar (see note)

3 hard-boiled eggs, peeled, yolks and whites separated and finely chopped or grated

1/2 cup (4 oz/125 g) crème fraîche

1/3 cup (1/2 oz/15 g) snipped fresh chives or 1/3 cup (2 oz/60 g) minced white onion

10 thin slices challah or brioche, crusts removed and toasted on both sides

SMOKED SALMON PINWHEELS

Festive occasions, like New Year's Eve, call for smoked salmon in some form. Here, it is rolled up in a thin, delicate crepe and sliced, and then each piece is topped with a small mound of bright orange salmon roe.

To make the batter, in a blender, combine the egg, milk, flour, butter, and a pinch of salt and process until smooth, about 30 seconds. Transfer the batter to a bowl and stir in the green onions. Cover the bowl with plastic wrap and refrigerate for at least 4 hours or for up to overnight.

Remove the batter from the refrigerator and let come to room temperature before cooking, about 30 minutes. Stir the batter gently to redistribute the green onions.

Preheat a nonstick 10-inch (25-cm) crepe pan or frying pan over medium heat. Using a pastry brush, lightly coat the pan with melted butter. Lift the pan from the heat and hold it at a slight angle. Pour ¼ cup (2 fl oz/60 ml) of the batter into the pan and tip and swirl the pan to cover the bottom evenly. Cook until the batter is almost dry and the edges have started to brown, about 1 minute. Using a wooden spatula, flip the crepe and cook until slightly browned on the second side and set, about 30 seconds longer. Transfer the crepe to a baking sheet and cover with a sheet of waxed paper. Repeat with the remaining batter to create 4 perfect crepes. Let cool to room temperature. (The cooked crepes can be stacked with waxed paper separating them, wrapped in plastic wrap, and refrigerated for up to 2 days.)

Lay the 4 crepes out on a work surface. Spread one-fourth of the cream cheese evenly over the surface of each crepe, leaving a ½-inch (12-mm) border uncovered around the entire edge. Lay one-fourth of the salmon strips over each cheese-topped crepe. Starting with the edge closest to you, tightly roll up each crepe into a cylinder. Wrap each crepe in plastic wrap and refrigerate for at least 1 hour or for up to 4 hours before serving.

Leaving the plastic wrap in place to help hold the rolled crepe together, and using a serrated knife, trim off ½ inch (12 mm) from each end of 1 rolled crepe. Slice the crepe crosswise into 6 equal pieces. Remove the plastic from each piece and arrange the pieces, spiral side facing up, on a tray. Repeat with the remaining rolled crepes. Top each piece with ½ teaspoon salmon roe and a dill sprig. Serve at once.

Serves 10

CREPE BATTER

1 large egg

½ cup (4 fl oz/125 ml) whole milk

½ cup (2½ oz/75 g) all-purpose (plain) flour

1 tablespoon unsalted butter, melted

Salt

3 green (spring) onions, including tender green tops, finely chopped

Melted unsalted butter for cooking

4 oz (125 g) cream cheese, at room temperature

4 oz (125 g) thinly sliced smoked salmon or gravlax, cut into strips 4 inches (10 cm) long and ¼ inch (6 mm) wide

¼ cup (2 oz/60 g) salmon roe

24 small fresh dill sprigs

LEMONGRASS SHRIMP SKEWERS

The lemongrass skewers used here contribute not only flavor to the shrimp, but also visual interest. Look for lemongrass in an Asian market or well-stocked food store.

Position a rack in the upper third of the oven and preheat to 400°F (200°C). Line a baking sheet with parchment (baking) paper. Drain the lemongrass stalks. Cut off the leafy tops from each stalk, leaving a 4-inch (10-cm) base intact. Cut each base lengthwise into quarters.

In a bowl, combine the shrimp and peanut sauce and toss until the shrimp are evenly coated. Using a metal skewer, make a small hole through the center of the thickest section of each shrimp. Thread 2 shrimp onto each of the lemongrass pieces. (You can prepare the skewers up to this point the night before, cover them with plastic wrap, and refrigerate until ready to cook.) Arrange the skewers on a baking sheet. Sprinkle the shrimp evenly with the peanuts and coconut.

Roast the shrimp until just opaque throughout, about 7 minutes. Remove from the oven and arrange the shrimp on a platter. Serve at once.

6 lemongrass stalks or 24 small wooden skewers, soaked in water for 10 minutes

48 medium shrimp (prawns), peeled and deveined

1/4 cup (2 fl oz/60 ml) store-bought Asian peanut sauce

3 tablespoons finely chopped dry-roasted peanuts

3 tablespoons unsweetened shredded coconut

TUNA TARTARE ON FLAT BREAD

The freshness of the fish is critical here, so ask your fishmonger for a piece of sushi-grade ahi, or yellowfin tuna. Look for the wasabi, sesame oil, and other Asian products in an Asian store or well-stocked supermarket.

Run your fingers over the tuna fillet to check for errant bones, and remove any you find with needle-nosed pliers. Cut the tuna into 1/4-inch (6-mm) cubes. In a nonreactive bowl, whisk together the lime juice, sesame oil, wasabi, soy sauce, and ginger. Add the tuna, chopped cilantro, and chives and toss to combine. (The tartare can be prepared up to 2 hours in advance, covered, and refrigerated.)

When ready to serve, mound about 1 tablespoon of the tartare mixture on each of the flat bread pieces. Garnish each mound with a cilantro leaf. Arrange the topped flat bread on a tray and serve at once.

Each recipe serves 10

1 lb (500 g) ahi tuna fillet

1 tablespoon fresh lime juice

2 teaspoons Asian sesame oil

1 teaspoon wasabi paste

2 teaspoons soy sauce

1 teaspoon peeled and grated fresh ginger

1 tablespoon chopped fresh cilantro (fresh coriander), plus 24 whole leaves for garnish

1 tablespoon snipped fresh chives

24 pieces sesame-seed flat bread, each about 2 inches (5 cm) square, or 24 square sesame-seed crackers

Beef Tenderloin Canapés

When you host a cocktail party, a menu with a selection of hors d'oeuvres that can be prepared in advance, such as this easy canapé recipe, is essential. If you like, put the cooked tenderloin in the freezer for about 15 minutes to make slicing it easier.

1¹/₂-lb (750-g) piece beef tenderloin, trimmed of fat and sinew

1 tablespoon chopped brined green peppercorns

1 tablespoon chopped fresh tarragon

2 green (spring) onions, including tender green tops, chopped, plus sliced green onion for garnish

Coarse salt

3 tablespoons olive oil

24 baguette slices, ¹/₄ inch (6 mm) thick

HORSERADISH CREAM

¹/₂ cup (4 oz/125 g) whipped cream cheese, at room temperature

2 tablespoons prepared horseradish

Remove the beef from the refrigerator about 30 minutes before you cook it, and preheat the oven to 400°F (200°C). In a small bowl, stir together the green peppercorns, tarragon, chopped green onions, and ¹/₂ teaspoon salt. Spread the mixture out on a plate large enough to hold the beef. Brush 1 tablespoon of the olive oil on all sides of the beef fillet. Roll the fillet in the green peppercorn mixture, pressing lightly so that it adheres to the surface.

In a large, ovenproof nonstick frying pan over high heat, warm the remaining 2 tablespoons olive oil. Add the beef and sear until evenly browned on all sides, 3–4 minutes. Place in the oven and cook until an instant-read thermometer inserted into the thickest part of the fillet registers 130°F (54°C) for medium-rare, 8–10 minutes. Transfer the beef to a piece of aluminum foil and let cool to room temperature. Wrap the beef in the foil and refrigerate for at least 4 hours or for up to overnight.

Reduce the oven temperature to 300°F (150°C). Arrange the baguette slices in a single layer on a rimmed baking sheet. Place in the oven and toast, turning occasionally, until golden brown on both sides, 15–20 minutes total. Remove from the oven and let cool. (The toasts can be stored in an airtight container at room temperature overnight.)

To make the horseradish cream, in a small bowl, whisk together the cream cheese and horseradish. (The cream can be stored in the refrigerator overnight; bring to room temperature before using.)

Remove the beef from the refrigerator, unwrap, and slice against the grain as thinly as possible. Spread an equal amount of the horseradish cream on each of the toasts. Place a slice or two of the beef on top of the cream cheese. Garnish each canapé with a few slices of green onion. Arrange the canapés on a tray and serve at once.

Serves 10

FRUIT TARTLETS

Prepared miniature tartlet shells are sold packaged in boxes at specialty-food stores. You can fill the shells with your favorite fruit preserves or citrus curd and top them with a simple garnish only minutes before serving. Be creative and fill and garnish the tartlets in a variety of ways.

To make the cranberry tartlets, in a small, dry frying pan over medium heat, toast the pecan pieces, shaking the pan often, until they start to brown and smell aromatic, about 7 minutes. Transfer to a small dish. Place the tartlet shells on a work surface and fill each shell with about 1 tablespoon of the cranberry preserves. Garnish each tartlet with a pecan piece and an orange zest strip.

To make the fig tartlets, place tartlet shells on a work surface and fill each shell with about 1 tablespoon of the fig preserves. Garnish each tartlet with a fig slice.

To make the lemon tartlets, place the tartlet shells on a work surface and fill each shell with about 1 tablespoon of the lemon curd. Garnish each tartlet with a raspberry and a mint leaf.

Arrange the tartlets on a serving tray and serve at once.

Serves 10

CRANBERRY TARTLETS

8 pecan pieces

8 prepared tartlet shells, each
1¹/₂ inches (4 cm) in diameter

¹/₂ cup (5 oz/155 g) cranberry preserves

8 thin orange zest strips

FIG TARTLETS

8 prepared tartlet shells, each
1¹/₂ inches (4 cm) in diameter

¹/₂ cup (5 oz/155 g) fig preserves

1 or 2 fresh ripe figs or plump dried
figs, cut into 8 thin wedges

LEMON TARTLETS

8 prepared tartlet shells, each
1¹/₂ inches (4 cm) in diameter

¹/₂ cup (5 oz/155 g) lemon curd

8 fresh raspberries

8 small fresh mint leaves

VALENTINE'S DAY DINNER FOR TWO

A simple way to create a romantic mood for an intimate dinner is to give it a change of scene. Here, two places are set at a low coffee table in front of the hearth, where the glow of firelight and candlelight provide soft, flattering illumination. Seated on comfortable cushions on the floor, you share an easy, casual, yet elegant menu.

A tall vase brimming with pink roses sits on the floor next to the table, adding color without overwhelming the setting. A luscious chocolate dessert makes a sweet ending to the cozy fireside meal.

MENU

Champagne

*Crab, Avocado, and Grapefruit Salad with
Chive Vinaigrette*

Pink Peppercorn Rack of Lamb

Roasted Yukon Gold Potatoes

Chocolate Crème Brûlée

WORK PLAN

AT LEAST ONE DAY IN ADVANCE

Make the chive oil for the salad

Bake the crème brûlée custards

THE DAY OF THE PARTY

Make the vinaigrette for the salad

JUST BEFORE SERVING

Assemble the salad

Roast the lamb and potatoes

Caramelize the crème brûlée custards

TIPS FOR INTIMATE DINING

- Choose recipes that do not require a lot of last-minute time in the kitchen.

- Buy half bottles (12 fl oz/375 ml) of wine if you want to serve both white and red wine with the meal.

- Remember to unplug the phone before sitting down to eat.

- Select relaxing music ahead of time so you will not need to get up from the table to adjust it.

EDIBLE VALENTINES

Add a romantic touch to the table by creating homemade chocolate "kisses," whimsical packages that contain a chocolate truffle and a love note. Set them in a bowl on the table, and put your favorite one on your valentine's plate.

gather the supplies you will need: store-bought chocolate truffles or other candies, squares of tissue paper cut with pinking shears to create a decorative edge, colorful ribbon, narrow strips of vellum or other paper, and a red pen.

wrap a truffle in each tissue-paper square, taking care not to stain the paper with the chocolate. Twist the ends of each packet to resemble a candy wrapper.

decorate each kiss by tying a small piece of ribbon on each end and tucking a message, written on strips of paper with red pen, under the edge of the tissue wrapper.

chill the Champagne thoroughly in a bucket filled with ice and water for about 20 minutes. If the Champagne is not cold enough, the cork is more likely to pop unexpectedly as you release it.

remove the foil covering from the top of the bottle, then twist open and remove the wire cage, keeping one hand firmly on the cork to prevent it from popping out before you are ready.

twist the bottle slowly with one hand, while grasping the cork firmly with the other hand. As you do this, hold the bottle at a 45-degree angle, pointing the cork away from you and others. If desired, cover the cork with a dish towel to give you a tighter grip and help manage any spills.

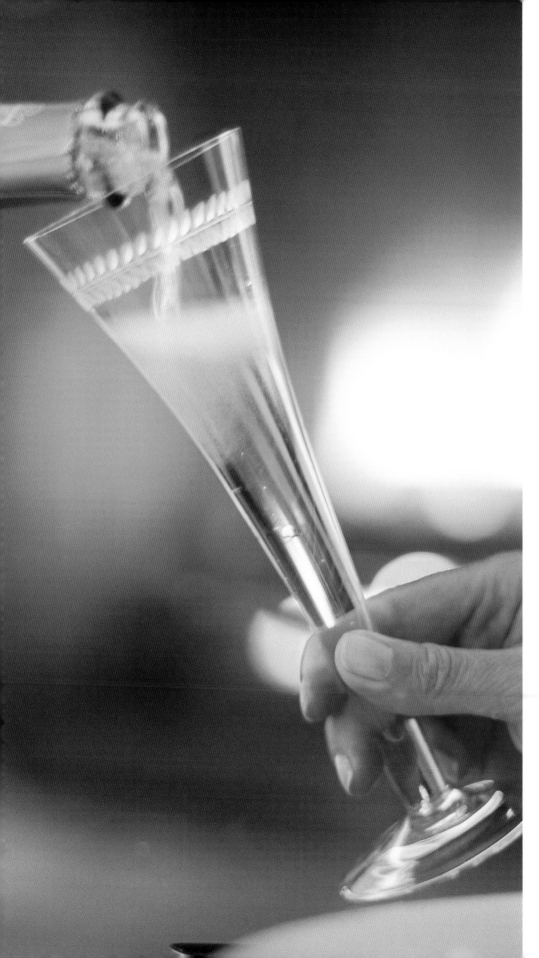

OPENING CHAMPAGNE

Popping the cork of a bottle of Champagne or sparkling wine might seem festive, but the sudden release of pressure usually causes the wine to overflow. A properly opened bottle should hiss, not pop, as the cork is slowly released.

CRAB, AVOCADO, AND GRAPEFRUIT SALAD WITH CHIVE VINAIGRETTE

Crabmeat from a freshly cooked crab is available during crab season at many seafood counters. Dungeness crabmeat is recommended here, but you can substitute any good-quality lump crabmeat, such as king or spider crab. Save any leftover chive oil to use on other salads.

To make the vinaigrette, combine the olive oil and the snipped chives in a blender and blend until smooth. Pour out ¹⁄₄ cup (2 fl oz/60 ml) to use in the vinaigrette. Set the remaining chive oil aside. In a small bowl, whisk together the crème fraîche, mustard, vinegar, and lemon juice. Slowly add the ¹⁄₄ cup chive oil while whisking constantly. Season to taste with salt and pepper.

In a bowl, combine the crabmeat, celery, and 3 tablespoons of the vinaigrette and stir gently to mix. In another bowl, toss together the avocado and lemon juice. Set both bowls aside.

Using a small, sharp knife, cut a slice off both ends of the grapefruit to reveal the flesh. Stand the grapefruit upright on a cutting board and, using the knife, thickly slice off the peel and pith in strips, cutting downward and following the contour of the fruit. Holding the grapefruit in one hand over a bowl, cut along either side of each section to release it from the membrane, letting the sections drop into the bowl. Pour any juice that collects in the bowl into the remaining vinaigrette.

To assemble the salad, add the crab mixture, avocado slices with lemon juice, and 2 tablespoons of the vinaigrette to the grapefruit sections, and toss to mix. Season to taste with salt and pepper.

Make a bed of the frisée and radicchio on chilled salad plates. Mound half of the crab salad in the center of each plate. Drizzle with the remaining vinaigrette. Top each salad with a few drops of the reserved chive oil. (Cap the remaining chive oil and reserve for another use. It will keep, tightly closed, for up to 2 weeks.) Scatter the chive pieces over the top and serve immediately.

Serves 2

CHIVE VINAIGRETTE

1 cup (8 fl oz/250 ml) olive oil

¹⁄₂ cup (³⁄₄ oz/20 g) snipped
fresh chives

2 tablespoons crème fraîche

2 teaspoons Dijon mustard

1 tablespoon Champagne vinegar

1 tablespoon fresh lemon juice

Coarse salt and freshly ground pepper

¹⁄₂ lb (250 g) Dungeness jumbo lump
crabmeat, picked over for cartilage
and shell fragments

1 tablespoon finely chopped celery

1 avocado, halved, pitted, peeled,
and sliced

Juice of ¹⁄₂ lemon

1 pink grapefruit

Coarse salt and freshly ground pepper

2 cups (3 oz/90 g) mixed torn frisée
and radicchio leaves

¹⁄₄ cup (¹⁄₄ oz/7 g) fresh chive pieces
(1-inch/2.5-cm lengths)

PINK PEPPERCORN RACK OF LAMB

Rack of lamb is easy to prepare and makes a sophisticated centerpiece for any menu. When ordering the rack, ask the butcher to "french" the ribs, that is, to cut away the meat from the end of the chops. Buttered green beans would be a nice vegetable to accompany the lamb.

1 rack of lamb, about 1¹/₂–1³/₄ lb (750–875 g), frenched (see note) with 6 or 8 ribs

1 tablespoon whole-grain Dijon mustard

2 tablespoons fine dried bread crumbs

1 tablespoon pink peppercorns, crushed

1 tablespoon chopped fresh rosemary

1 clove garlic, minced

Coarse salt

¹/₄ cup (2 fl oz/60 ml) extra-virgin olive oil

¹/₃ cup (3 fl oz/80 ml) dry white wine

Preheat the oven to 400°F (200°C). Rub the fat side of the rack of lamb with the mustard and set aside. In a small bowl, stir together the bread crumbs, peppercorns, rosemary, garlic, and 1 teaspoon salt. Lightly pat the bread crumb mixture evenly over the mustard layer so that it adheres to the surface.

In a nonstick, ovenproof frying pan, warm the olive oil over medium heat. Add the lamb and sear on all sides until lightly golden, about 3 minutes per side. Position the rack fat side up and place in the oven. Roast until browned and cooked to your liking, 13–15 minutes for medium-rare. Remove from the oven, transfer the lamb to a cutting board, tent with aluminum foil, and let rest for 10 minutes.

Return the frying pan to the stove top over medium heat. Add the wine, scraping up any brown bits from the pan bottom. Pour the pan juices through a fine-mesh sieve placed over a bowl. To serve, cut the rack apart into chops, and divide the chops evenly among warmed individual plates. Spoon the pan juices over the chops. Serve at once.

ROASTED YUKON GOLD POTATOES

Yukon gold potatoes, with their thin skins and buttery flesh, take well to oven roasting. Here, they are tossed with only a little lemon juice, olive oil, salt, and pepper before roasting to a rich golden brown.

³/₄ lb (375 g) Yukon gold potatoes, each about 1–1¹/₂ inches (2.5–4 cm) in diameter, cut in half crosswise

1 tablespoon fresh lemon juice

2 tablespoons olive oil

Coarse salt and freshly ground pepper

Preheat the oven to 400°F (200°C). In a bowl, toss together the potatoes, lemon juice, and olive oil until evenly coated. Season with salt and pepper. Transfer the potatoes to a baking dish large enough to hold them in a single layer. Roast the potatoes for 15 minutes. Stir the potatoes and continue to roast until golden brown and tender when pierced with a fork, 15–20 minutes longer. Serve warm.

Each recipe serves 2

Chocolate Crème Brûlée

For special occasions, use a ramekin that has a decorative shape and color, or nestle a simple white ramekin into a folded colored napkin that complements your table. If desired, accompany this rich, satisfying dessert with a few fresh raspberries and thin sugar cookies.

Preheat the oven to 325°F (165°C). Select a baking pan large enough to hold two ³/₄-cup (6–fl oz/180 ml) ramekins and line it with a kitchen towel.

In a saucepan over medium heat, combine the cream and the vanilla bean and bring slowly to a gentle simmer. Remove from the heat and retrieve the vanilla bean halves. Using the tip of a small knife, scrape the seeds from each half into the cream. Discard the bean halves. Add the chocolate and stir until melted and well combined. Set the pan aside.

In a bowl, whisk together the egg yolks, 3 tablespoons of the superfine sugar, and a pinch of salt until thick and creamy, about 2 minutes. Slowly add the warm cream mixture while whisking constantly. Pour the custard through a fine-mesh sieve into a pitcher. Fill each ramekin almost to the top and place the ramekins in the prepared baking dish. Pour boiling water into the dish to reach halfway up the sides of the ramekins. Cover the baking dish loosely with aluminum foil.

Bake the custards until they start to set around the edges, but the centers still wiggle when a ramekin is gently shaken, 20–25 minutes. Remove the ramekins from the baking dish and set aside on a wire rack to cool for 1 hour. Cover and refrigerate for at least 3 hours or for up to overnight.

When ready to serve, have ready a kitchen propane torch or preheat a broiler (grill). Sprinkle the top of each ramekin evenly with 1 tablespoon of the remaining sugar. If using a kitchen torch, pass it closely over the sugar-topped custards to melt and caramelize the sugar. If using the broiler, place the custards on a baking sheet and slip under the broiler 4 inches (10 cm) from the heat source. Broil (grill) until the sugar melts and caramelizes, 1–2 minutes. The top of each custard should be a dark caramel color, brittle, and warm, while the custard itself should remain cool. Serve at once.

Serves 2

1 cup (8 fl oz/250 ml) heavy (double) cream

¹/₂ vanilla bean, split lengthwise

2 oz (60 g) semisweet (plain) chocolate, coarsely chopped

2 large egg yolks

5 tablespoons (2¹/₂ oz/75 g) superfine (caster) sugar

Salt

ELEMENTS OF THE TABLE

How you choose to set and adorn the table contributes to the overall mood of any party. When selecting the elements that will transform an everyday table into a festive one, it is helpful to divide them into five categories: dinnerware, glassware, flatware, linens, and decorative elements.

Dinnerware

On a spectrum ranging from homespun to refined, most dinnerware falls into one of five types: pottery, earthenware, stoneware, porcelain, and bone china. However, you should never feel obliged to match the formality of the occasion with the dinnerware. Even a relatively formal table does not require fine china, and elegant plates might be just right for a casual supper. It is more important to use pieces that are complementary and remain consistent to one style. In other words, use either pottery or porcelain dishes, but avoid mixing the two. Cultivate a collection of basic white dinnerware. Supplemented with colorful accent pieces, it is an ideal choice for most occasions. If possible, use matching plates for each course, even if you cannot match them from one course to the next. Count the pieces you plan to use well ahead of time to be sure you have enough of each type. If you do not, buy or borrow more as needed.

Glassware

As with dinnerware, it is not necessary for all your glasses to match. What is critical is that they be of similar quality and style. Simple, clear glassware is always an appropriate choice. Although you can augment your collection with some colored pieces, for the most part, avoid colored stemware, which can mask or clash with the color of the wine. See Serving Wine (page 311) for guidelines about which kinds of stemware to use for various types of wine. If you have crystal, you do not need to reserve it for fancy occasions. The sparkle of crystal can liven up even the simplest, most casual table setting.

Flatware

Again, matching flatware pieces is of less consequence than consistency of quality and style. Start with a basic set of silver-toned flatware. For a feeling of heirloom quality and a satisfying heft, there is nothing like sterling silver. But because it must be washed by hand and requires a fair amount of maintenance, it is usually reserved for special occasions. Silver plate is less expensive, but also needs special care. Good-quality stainless steel is an appropriate choice for most occasions. It is easy to maintain and, unlike silver, can be washed in the dishwasher. Look for heavy pieces

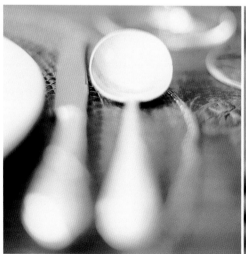

with thick handles and simple, timeless designs. To add to your collection, scour secondhand stores and flea markets for antique or hotel flatware.

Linens

A simple, high-quality cotton or linen tablecloth and napkins in white or cream tones are a good starting point for both casual and formal table settings. Before choosing a tablecloth, measure your table and allow for an 18-inch (45-cm) overhang, which will drape attractively without interfering with diners' legs. Use a white cloth on its own or as a liner beneath a colored or translucent cloth. Tablecloths are often reserved for formal occasions, but they can be used instead of the more typical place mats to add style to casual dining as well. If the tablecloth has a few crisp creases, try to align them with the center and sides of the dining table to make them less obvious. Consider table runners, too, for adorning a dining table. These long, thin strips of fabric can add a nice splash of color to a bare wood table.

Cloth napkins—even simple ones— should be used whenever possible. If they are monogrammed, fold them so that the monogram is on the lower left-hand corner or the center of the bottom of the napkin. Tradition holds that a napkin is placed either to the left of the forks or on top of the plate. However, these days many hosts opt to put the napkin under the forks, especially at informal events or when space is at a premium. For formal table settings, the napkins and tablecloth should match.

For casual dining, they can either match or complement each other.

Decorative Elements

Collect an assortment of small, simply designed vases in neutral colors to decorate the table. To help anchor flowers, use clear marbles, frogs, sea glass, or other decorative objects—even citrus fruits (see page 26). Consider using a variety of containers— cordial glasses, compote cups, small pails— as vases to add extra flair.

Centerpieces create a decorative focal point. But remember, less is more. A centerpiece should not overwhelm the table or obstruct sight lines, so keep it low and relatively simple.

To arrange flowers, cut the stems on the diagonal to help them absorb water. Stripping the leaves below the water line will help keep the arrangement fresh and the water clear. If possible, keep the flowers out of direct sunlight to prolong their life.

Flowers are the most popular choice for a centerpiece, but other objects also work well. For example, put together a bowl of seasonal fruits or vegetables that reflect some element of the menu. If you use flowers, avoid blooms with a strong fragrance that will compete with the food.

"Satellites" are small matching arrangements of flowers or other items that can be placed around the room to create multiple focal points and to tie together the decor. They can be put at individual place settings, clustered together to make a centerpiece, or lined up along the length of the table to produce a "runner" effect.

Candles should be either short, such as votive candles, or tall enough so that the flame is above the heads of the diners. White or cream-colored candles are suitable for any occasion. Regardless of color, however, they should be unscented and dripless. Candles are not generally lit at daytime parties, but they can be used unlit in attractive candleholders as ornamental table accents.

Serving Wine

Once you have selected the wines that will accompany your meal, you need to think about how you will present them. A few simple principles about glassware, temperature, and serving can make a dramatic difference in bringing out the wine's best qualities.

If you will be serving more than one wine at a meal, your table setting should include an appropriate glass for each. Wait until the guests are seated before pouring wine, then fill glasses between one-third and one-half full. This allows room for the wine to breathe and for swirling it to bring out its full aroma. Serve sparkling wines very cold (42°–45°F/6°–7°C) as an aperitif, with the first course, or with dessert. White wines should be chilled to 45°–50°F (7°–10°C); if they are too cold or too warm, their flavor will be dulled. Reds and most dessert wines are best served at cool room temperature.

Wine can, of course, be served in any kind of glass, but good wineglasses are specially designed to showcase a wine's character and enhance enjoyment. They have stems to keep the heat of your hand

An example of basic wineglass shapes: Champagne or sparkling wine flute, white-wine glass, Burgundy glass, Bordeaux glass, Port or dessert-wine glass

Setting the Table

Before you begin planning your table setting, give some thought to the table itself. Will it be large enough to accommodate all of your guests comfortably? Ideally, you should allow about 2 feet (60 cm) of space from the center of one plate to the center of the next, especially for more formal seated gatherings.

Whether your party is casual or formal, you do not need to be an interior designer to create an attractive, inviting table. When in doubt, err on the side of simplicity: Start with white and then add a few accents of color. Avoid overdecorating, and you will find that the flatware and glassware will add plenty of sparkle to the scene.

The Informal Table

A casual table setting reflects the simplicity of the meal to come. Select a no-frills tablecloth or place mats, and use matching or complementary cotton napkins. Everyday flatware, dishes, and glassware are appropriate, and can be augmented with a few special pieces.

The idea of table-setting guidelines might seem at odds with the spirit of a casual dinner. But these conventions, far from being arbitrary rules of style, are intended to make the meal a more comfortable and enjoyable experience for your guests.

For each guest, put a napkin on top of or to the left of the plate, folded side facing the plate, allowing space to its right for the forks. Arrange all flatware in the order in which it will be used, starting from the outermost item. To the right of the napkin,

from affecting the temperature of the wine, and their bowls are shaped to maximize flavor and aroma.

When buying stemware, look for thin-walled glasses that have a cut and polished lip, and that feel substantial in your hand. Wineglasses come in a wide variety of sizes, shapes, and designs, but you need only four kinds for a basic collection: sparkling wine flutes, white-wine glasses, red-wine glasses, and dessert-wine glasses.

Flutes are used to serve Champagne and other sparkling wines. Their tall, narrow shape reduces the wine's surface area, keeping the bubbles from dissipating and enhancing their effervescence.

White-wine glasses are tulip shaped, with a tapered top to concentrate the aroma. When buying them, look for a large bowl with ample room to swirl the wine and savor its bouquet. If you are just beginning to acquire wineglasses, start with these,

because they also can be used for serving red wine.

Red-wine glasses are similar to white-wine glasses, but larger. In general, the bigger the personality of the wine, the bigger the glass should be. Burgundy glasses are bubble shaped, with a wide bowl designed to bring out the complexity of the wine and make the most of its aroma. They are ideal for lighter reds with more delicate aromas, such as Pinot Noir. These glasses can also be used for elegant white Burgundies. The larger Bordeaux glass, with straight sides that allow more air to be incorporated into the wine, is best suited for more robust wines, such as Cabernet Sauvignon. If you are buying your first set of red-wine glasses, choose a medium size and straight sides.

Dessert-wine or Port glasses mimic the shape of wineglasses, but they are not as big because such high-alcohol and fortified wines are served in smaller portions.

put a salad fork if you are serving an appetizer or salad course. A larger, main-course fork goes to the right of the salad fork. The knife should be placed to the right of the plate, its blade facing inward. If you are serving soup, set the soup spoon to the right of the knife, since most people hold the spoon with their right hand.

Next, set a water glass above the knife; then, to its right, place a wineglass. There is no need to lay out bread knives, bread plates, dessert implements, or teaspoons at a casual meal. Guests can put bread directly on their dinner plate or on the tablecloth; forks or spoons for dessert can be brought out along with the dessert, and teaspoons with the tea or coffee.

The Formal Table

A successful formal table setting is more about "special occasion" than about "formality." This is the time and place to bring out the best—fine china, linen tablecloth and napkins, good silver and glassware—and to take the time and care to place every piece to its greatest advantage. The effect of the table should be one of harmonious and inviting elegance, not ostentation.

At a formal meal, there should always be a plate in front of each guest. A charger, or large service plate, is typically used as a placeholder in creating the initial table setting. It remains on the table through the first course or courses, under the smaller plates on which those dishes are served. The charger both showcases these opening offerings and protects the table linen. The charger is removed from the table when the main course is served.

The napkin goes to the left of the setting, folded side facing the plate, ready to be picked up and laid across the lap as the guest sits down. It can also be centered on the plate, especially if it is folded in a decorative way. Some hosts choose to place the napkin between the charger and the small plate for a decorative touch.

Place forks to the right of the napkin in the order in which they will be used, starting from the outside and progressing inward toward the plate. If salad is served after the main course, put the salad fork to the right of the main-course fork.

Set the main-course knife to the right of the plate, its blade facing inward, ready for the guest to pick it up for cutting. Lay the dessert silverware just above the plate, the handle of the spoon pointing to the right and the handle of the fork to the left. If space is tight, these pieces can be omitted from the table and brought out with dessert. Position a small bread plate to the left of the forks, or just above them if space is an issue. Across its upper rim, lay a butter knife, its handle facing to the right and its blade facing the center of the plate.

Each place setting should include all of the glassware that will be needed for the meal, arranged in a diagonal line above the knife, in order of use from closest to farthest. Place a white-wine glass, which is typically used with the first course, just above the tip of the knife. Diagonally up and to its left, put a larger glass for red wine, which is traditionally served with

Informal table setting: Everyday flatware, a plain white plate, and an all-purpose glass for water or wine. Place mats can stand in for a tablecloth.

Formal table setting: Special-occasion flatware and an optional charger. Wine and water glasses are arranged at an angle above the knife.

the main course. Diagonally up and to the left, place an even larger glass or goblet for water. This order can vary depending on the order and types of wine to be served, but always set the water glass in the leftmost position.

Set out one set of salt and pepper shakers, cellars, or grinders for every two to four guests. Be sure to fill pepper grinders with fresh whole peppercorns. Cellars should be outfitted with small serving spoons.

The Buffet

A buffet should convey abundance. Choose a table or sideboard that will be just the right size to hold everything. If it is too small, it can be difficult to manage, and if it is too large, it can look sparse and uninviting. Set the serving platters on the buffet ahead of time to get a sense of their spacing and placement.

If space allows, pull the table or sideboard out into the room so guests can serve themselves from both sides. For large buffets, consider dividing each dish between two similar platters and creating a mirrored effect down the sides of the table.

Cover the surface of the buffet with a tablecloth, or use a runner or place mats. Once you have determined what the traffic flow will be, set the plates at the beginning of the buffet and the napkins and utensils at the end. That way the guests will not have to juggle them while they fill their plates. To make serving easier, roll the utensils in the napkins so that they are easy to pick up and carry to the eating area. Alternatively, set silverware and napkins at the dining table or tables. The latter is a nice touch for more formal occasions.

Arrange the food in the order in which it will be eaten: first course, main course, side dishes, and so on. Remember to put out appropriate serving utensils for each dish. Put cold dishes before hot ones, and carved meat toward the end of the buffet. Carve meat for each guest, rather than have

the guests carve their own, to keep the buffet line moving at a nice pace.

Setting up a separate table for desserts—or re-setting the buffet once the meal has been served—will also help make service more efficient. Designate another table for drinks (see Basic Bar Checklist, page 13), and place it as far from the main buffet as possible to keep traffic flowing.

Placing food at different heights on the buffet table creates an attractive look and makes serving easier. It can also help you fit more food on a smaller table. To elevate dishes, use pedestals or footed bowls, or place platters on boxes or bowls set under the tablecloth or draped with napkins.

Once the buffet setting has been worked out, you can add some decorative touches. If you are using a centerpiece, make sure it will not interfere with serving. Flowers with a mild fragrance are a good choice. Take care when using candles; some can be easily knocked over. The centerpiece can be placed in the middle of a two-sided buffet. For a one-sided buffet, arrange it against the wall or at one end of the table. You can also scatter small decorations or low, stable vases of flowers along the entire length of the buffet table or sideboard.

As the meal progresses, keep an eye on the food, and replenish or replace platters as needed. Having extra prearranged platters and garnishes ready in the kitchen makes it easy to keep everything on the table looking and tasting fresh. Unless you have a warming plate or chafing dish, it is wise to serve dishes on the buffet that taste good at room temperature.

INDEX

ACKNOWLEDGMENTS

WELDON OWEN wishes to thank the following individuals and organizations for their kind assistance: Desne Ahlers, Birdman Inc., Emma Boys, Carrie Bradley, Kimberly Chun, Ken DellaPenta, Julia Flagg, Sharon Silva, Colin Wheatland, The Blackwell Files, table top by Cary Nowell, and Lynn Goldfinger-Abram.

GEORGE DOLESE would like to thank Elisabet der Nederlanden for testing, fine-tuning, and preparing each recipe beautifully for photography (you are the best); Hannah Rahill and Gaye Allen for the opportunity to author this book; Jennifer Newens for keeping me on track and her great editorial guidance; Amy Marr for organizing all the shoots and making sure we all had our vitamin C during flu season; Nicky Collings and Leslie Harrington, art directors, for taking this book to a higher level; Quentin Bacon for bringing life into the photography; Sara Slavin for adding a stylish flair to the table settings; Steve Siegelman for joining us and pulling his incredible literary thread through the book; Sharon Silva for helping put the obvious into words; Chris Stark and Val Cipollone for sharing their expertise on wine; Ver Brugge Meats for quality products and friendly service; Mike Gallin for the desk chair that made sitting at the computer for hours a comfortable experience; and my core group of friends, with whom I have had the pleasure of spending countless hours around the table; they know that nothing makes me happier. This book is dedicated in part to Marguerite and Jim Fitzgerald, who at an early age taught me the importance of sharing a meal at home with family and friends, which is what "Entertaining" is really about.

SARA SLAVIN wishes to extend a special thanks to several Bay Area businesses for generously providing many of the wonderful elements of the table that grace this book. Thank you to Dandelion, San Francisco; Heath Ceramics, Sausalito; Namoi's American Pottery, San Francisco; Kartell, San Francisco; and especially to Sue Fisher King, San Francisco, for their ongoing generosity and contribution to this book. She would also like to thank Amy, Jen, Gaye, Hannah, Nicky, Leslie, Quentin, and Elisabet, for all their support always; her assistant Brooke Buchanan, and especially George Dolese for beautiful, delicious food and extraordinary support throughout this project.

PHOTO CREDITS

QUENTIN BACON, all photography, except for the following:
MAREN CARUSO: Pages 4 (right), 6, 84–85, 86 (right), Garden Party chapter 106–25, 162 (left), Pizza Party chapter 164–79, except for the style tip on 170–71, which was shot by Quentin Bacon
PRUE RUSCOE: Pages 4 (left), 16–17, 20–21, 24 (left), 25 (left), 26–29, 34–35, 38 (center), 39, 41, 44–45, 47, 50, 52–53, 55 (lower right), 58–59, 64, 67–69

OXMOOR HOUSE INC.

Oxmoor
House®

Oxmoor House books are distributed by Sunset Books
80 Willow Road, Menlo Park, CA 94025
Telephone: 650-321-3600 Fax: 650-324-1532
Vice President/General Manager: Rich Smeby
National Accounts Manager/Special Sales: Brad Moses
Oxmoor House and Sunset Books are divisions of
Southern Progress Corporation

WILLIAMS-SONOMA, INC.

Founder & Vice-Chairman: Chuck Williams

THE ENTERTAINING SERIES

Conceived and produced by
WELDON OWEN INC.
814 Montgomery Street, San Francisco, CA 94133
Telephone: 415-291-0100 Fax: 415-291-8841

In Collaboration with Williams-Sonoma, Inc.
3250 Van Ness Avenue, San Francisco, CA 94109

A WELDON OWEN PRODUCTION

Copyright © 2004 Weldon Owen Inc.
and Williams-Sonoma, Inc.

All rights reserved, including the right of
reproduction in whole or in part in any form.

First printed in 2004
10 9 8 7 6 5 4

ISBN 0-8487-2781-9

Printed by Midas Printing Limited
Printed in China

WELDON OWEN INC.

Chief Executive Officer: John Owen

President and Chief Operating Officer: Terry Newell

VP International Sales: Stuart Laurence

Creative Director: Gaye Allen

Publisher: Hannah Rahill

Business Manager: Richard Van Oosterhout

Associate Publisher: Amy Marr

Senior Editor: Jennifer Newens

Assistant Editor: Donita Boles

Editorial Assistant: Juli Vendzules

Associate Creative Director: Leslie Harrington

Art Director: Nicky Collings

Designer: Karin Skaggs

Production Director: Chris Hemesath

Color Specialist: Teri Bell

Photographer's Assistants: William Moran and Nathan Murray

Assistant Food Stylist: Elisabet der Nederlanden

Assistant Prop Stylist: Brooke Buchanan